Through The Subarctic Forest

THROUGH
THE SUBARCTIC FOREST

A MONARCH OF THE FOREST.

A MONARCH OF THE DESERT.

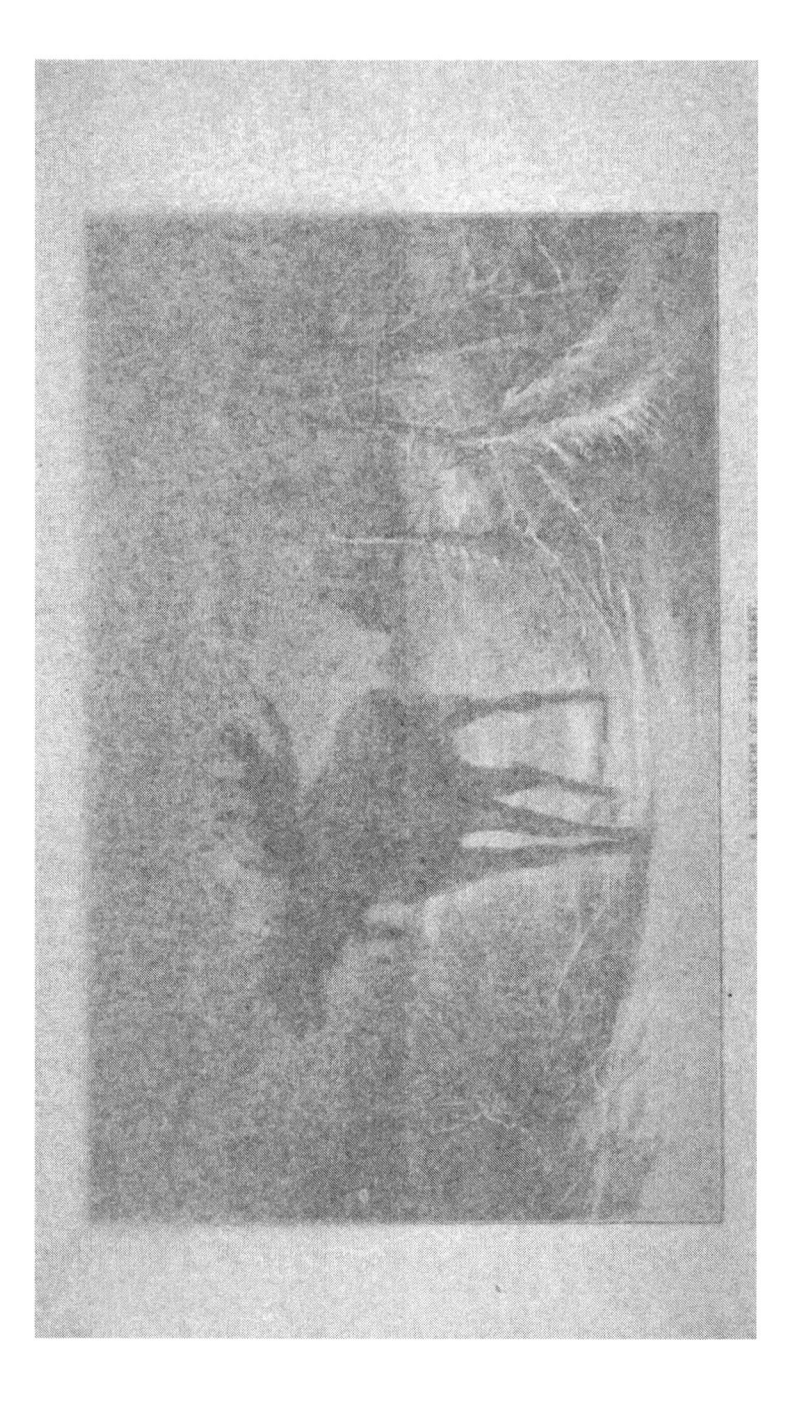

THROUGH THE SUBARCTIC FOREST

A RECORD OF A CANOE JOURNEY FROM FORT
WRANGEL TO THE PELLY LAKES AND
DOWN THE YUKON RIVER TO
THE BEHRING SEA

BY

WARBURTON PIKE

AUTHOR OF 'THE BARREN GROUNDS OF CANADA'

WITH ILLUSTRATIONS AND MAPS

EDWARD ARNOLD
Publisher to the India Office

LONDON
37 BEDFORD STREET

NEW YORK
70 FIFTH AVENUE

1896

1896, Oct. 31
Zoölogical Museum

PREFACE

IN the summer of 1887 an expedition was undertaken and successfully carried out by the Geological Survey Department of Canada, with a view to gathering some accurate knowledge of the little-known tracts of country adjacent to the northern waterways of the Dominion.

The expedition was conducted speedily and quietly, attracting little attention at the time, as the inhabitants of the well-settled portions of Canada hardly realised what an enormous amount of work was accomplished, and what long distances were covered in a comparatively short space of time by methods of travel which seem primeval to the creature of modern civilisation.

The result of all this work has been the correct mapping of several of the main routes through the vast territory over which the Hudson's Bay Company have always held sway, so that in many cases the traveller or hunter whose tastes drive him to the northern solitudes knows exactly what lies before him, knows when to look out for the rapids, and knows the distance between points of importance, instead of having to depend on the vague information afforded by Indians, who take little account of time or distance.

The first part of the journey which I have attempted to describe in the following pages, with the exception of the country lying to the northeast of a line drawn from the north end of Frances Lake to the site of the Old Pelly Banks trading post, which I believe to be absolutely new ground, lies chiefly along the route followed by the Exploratory Survey party under the leadership of Dr. G. M. Dawson, and in his Report will be found an interesting and accurate account of the country travelled through.

The only geographical discovery of any importance that I made was rather of a negative character, namely, that the river draining the Pelly Lakes, and marked as the Pelly on the maps prepared from Indian reports, is not really entitled to be considered the main stream of the Pelly, but is only a small tributary of a large river heading towards the north-east, and probably having its source on the western slope of the main range of the Rocky Mountains. I have made some attempt to map this hitherto unexplored tract of country, but the sketch must be regarded as only roughly approximate till a competent surveyor goes over the ground to correct the numerous errors.

To the sportsman and man of the woods, this book is offered as a rough description of what happened on a long journey through a good game country, without any attempt to make a big bag or killing animals that were not wanted to keep up the food supply. I have purposely dwelt more at length on the Pelly and Liard district, though lying nearer at hand, which is but really less known than the often-described country of the Yukon and the Behring Sea.

Rough geological and botanical collections were made in the course of the journey, and a description of them will be found in an appendix to this volume. They are not nearly so perfect as I could have wished, but allowance must be made for the fact that I was my own steersman and hunter, and my attention was often drawn from more scientific pursuits by the perils of navigation or the emptiness of the larder.

W. P.

CONTENTS

CHAPTER I

START FOR FORT WRANGEL

Coast line of British Columbia—Fort Wrangel and its history—Miners of '49—Laws of Alaska—The canoe and her requirements—Stikine River, difficulties of navigation—Iskoot tributary . . . 1

CHAPTER II

ON THE STIKINE RIVER

The Stikine glacier—Overtaken by coast Indians—Canoe drill at Little Cañon—Difference in climate on opposite sides of coast range—Salmon catching—Habits of bears—Klootchman Cañon—The Chinook jargon—Telegraph Creek—Freight charges . . 22

CHAPTER III

THE DISTRICT OF CASSIAR

Cassiar trail—Laketon—A Hudson Bay trading post—Dease Lake—Drawbacks to mining—Sylvester's Landing—Casca Indians—Abandon plan of wintering on Frances Lake . . . 50

CHAPTER IV

THE LIARD POST

Mount Ke-la-gurn—Hyland River—Indian superstitions—Big game in particular localities—First fall of snow 66

CHAPTER V

MOOSE HUNTING

The country south of Liard River—Civilised Indians—Increase of number of moose—Habits of the moose 84

CHAPTER VI

HAULING STORES TO FRANCES LAKE

Ice set fast in the rivers—Cassiar sleigh dogs—Disease among the Liard Indians—Ideal day for a hunt—Difficulties of hauling supplies—Dangers of a really cold day—A process of freezing out . 97

CHAPTER VII

A MINING EXPEDITION

Return to Sylvester's Landing for summer supplies—Rabbits and grouse—Murder by Casca Indians—Expedition to Hyland River—Quartz ledges—Chesi Hill, the home of the big-horn—Jealousy between Cassiar Indians and Red River half-breeds 110

CHAPTER VIII

START FOR THE PELLY RIVER

La Montagne's arrival on 18th April. The Liard chief's theory of the Unknown—Journey up Frances River—Frances Lake—The legend of the flying cariboo—Pelly Indians—Yus-ez-uh River—More stories of cannibals across the divide 124

CHAPTER IX

PTARMIGAN CREEK

The thaw—Geese and beaver—Macpherson Lake—The divide—Pelly Lake—Wild-fowl—A good place for winter quarters—Running the canoe down Ptarmigan Creek 141

CHAPTER X

EXPEDITION TOWARDS SOURCE OF PELLY RIVER

Disease among the rabbits—Swallows' nests—Drying fish—Upper Pelly Lake—Gull Lake—Ptarmigans nesting and signs of summer—Accident to rifle—A bad miss—Dogs go astray; their instinct . 158

CHAPTER XI

DOWN THE PELLY RIVER

Salmon a long distance from the sea—Claims of Pelly River to be considered main branch of Yukon—Scarcity of provisions—A cow moose—Slate Rapid—Hoole River—A grizzly bear and the result of a broken rifle 178

CHAPTER XII

DOWN THE PELLY AND YUKON RIVERS

Portage at Hoole Cañon—Varieties of mountain sheep—Ross River—Macmillan and Stewart Rivers—Difficulties of prospecting—Granite Cañon—Fort Selkirk—The Lewes River—First run of Salmon—Government officials and gamblers . . . 197

CHAPTER XIII

FORTY-MILE CREEK TO FORT YUKON

Forty-Mile Creek—Miners' law—Boundary line between Alaska and British Columbia—Arrival of the *Arctic*—Coal Creek—Ovis Dallii—The Yukon Flats—Route from Athabasca to Behring Sea . 218

CHAPTER XIV

THE KUSKOKVIM RIVER

Tanana River—Bones of the mastodon—Murder of Archbishop Seghers—Ikogmut—Kuskokvim River—A game country . . . 237

CHAPTER XV

ON SALT WATER

Coast navigation—The Innuits, their food, habits, and dress—Moses and Aaron—Good News Bay—A scene of desolation—Kayaks—Cape Newenham 253

CHAPTER XVI

VOYAGE TO OUNALASKA

A gale of wind—Karlukuk Bay—Inland navigation again—Wood River—The schooner, her skipper and crew of many nations—Ounalaska—Homeward bound in the 'Frisco steamer . . . 273

APPENDIX

I.—A List of Geological Specimens collected by Mr. Warburton Pike near the head-waters of the Pelly River . . . 287

II.—A List of Plants collected by Mr. Warburton Pike in Alaska and the North-West Territory of Canada 293

LIST OF ILLUSTRATIONS

A Monarch of the Forest	*Frontispiece*
	PAGE
Fort Wrangel	5
On the Stikine River	23
The Glenora Rapid	43
Dinner Camp *en route*	53
An Ideal Stream for Canoeing	73
A Winter Camp	87
Cow Moose Feeding	93
Burnt Timber in Winter	101
Break-up of Ice on the Frances River	129
Pelly Lake	149
Swallow Bluff	161
Pelly River at the Junction with Hoole River	191
He had given me enough chances	193
The Head of Hoole Cañon	199
Shooting a Rapid	205
Wild-fowl on the Yukon Flats	233
Map of the Pelly Lakes and Surrounding Districts	*To face page* 138
Map of Alaska showing the Author's Route	*At end*

CHAPTER I

START FOR FORT WRANGEL

Coast line of British Columbia—Fort Wrangel and its history—Miners of '49—Laws of Alaska—The canoe and her requirements—Stikine River, difficulties of navigation—Iskoot tributary.

ON a bright Sunday morning early in July 1892, we steamed out of the harbour of Victoria, Vancouver's Island, and before nightfall had left Vancouver — the thriving mainland town at the terminus of the Canadian Pacific Railway — far behind us. It is curious that this confusing name of Vancouver should have continued in use after it had once served its purpose in roughly locating the geographical position of the new city, and attracting the attention of land speculators; more especially as there is yet another Vancouver a couple of hundred miles farther south, on the banks of the Columbia River. It is too late now, I suppose, to alter the name; but it seems a pity that the memory of the old sea captain should be associated with the bricks and mortar of a new railway town, instead of with the rugged mountains and dense pine forests which rise in lonely grandeur from the waters of the Pacific.

After a four days' voyage through the rain-smeared islands that guard the gloomy coast-lines of British Columbia, with several calls at small settlements of little interest to any one but their inhabitants, we reached Fort Wrangel, a port of entry for the U.S. Territory of Alaska, situated on the west side of a thickly wooded island bearing the same name, about six miles from the mouth of the Stikine River.

Fort Wrangel's existence dates back as far as the year 1834, when it was established under the name of Fort Dionysius as a military station during the Russian occupancy of Alaska, to watch the proceedings of the Hudson's Bay Company, then trading on the Coast. Gold was discovered on the Stikine River in 1862; but Fort Wrangel's palmy days began with the rush of miners to the Cassiar District, on the Arctic Slope, which followed in 1874. But these good times are gone by, and the little town now presents a most desolate appearance, lacking all natural beauty to atone for the absence of prosperity, while the almost perpetual rainfall makes it an undesirable place of abode. The small white population is, however, made up of the right kind of people; and they treated us with all the hospitality that is so sure to be found among men who have spent much of their time in western mining camps.

Fort Wrangel seems to have become a resting-place for the type of pioneer who is now all too scarce on the Pacific coast—the man who has passed his life on the frontier, moving from California to Cariboo, Omeneca, Couer d'Alene, and Cassiar, as each new field was discovered. Possessed of a happy, careless nature, he has borne good and bad fortune with the same equanimity; he will tell you many a story of good claims sold for large sums of money, which always disappeared in one good spree in the nearest town, shared with his fellows as readily as ever was the last kettleful of beans in the mountains. Doubtless his conduct on these occasions was none too orderly, and his sins were committed with great rapidity while the spree lasted; but even so his record might show a much better average than that of many of the respectable hypocrites who are so easily shocked at the miner's excesses in times of prosperity. There is not a better-hearted fellow or a truer friend in time of need than a good specimen of the old class of genuine hard-working miners. But, alas! the days of '49 are gone, and our worthy friend has reached the time of life when the hardships of his youth begin to tell upon him, and his overworked knees will no longer do their duty. Too often he is encumbered with an Indian woman and a tribe of half-breed children—a state of affairs which has dragged many a good man down to a lower social level than he was intended to fill; and every year makes it harder for him to leave the semi-civilisation of the coast and plunge into the wilderness in search of the one more stake that is all he has to depend upon for the comfort of his declining years. But the younger part of the mining population has been drawn away to the new town of Juneau, a little farther up the coast, and close to the celebrated treadmill mine on Douglas Island —the only really paying mine in Alaska, whose reputation has been freely used to bolster up several rotten enterprises started on claims in close proximity to the Bonanza. So Wrangel is now almost

FORT WRANGEL.

entirely supported by the Indian trade, which is still of some importance. A sawmill has been built to supply the local market; but the export of lumber, which might under favourable legislation develop into a larger industry, is forbidden.

The laws in force throughout Alaska are of the most unsatisfactory kind, and apparently no means are taken to improve them. So far no land titles of any sort have been granted, and a man who builds himself a house does so without the least guarantee that the land on which he builds it will ever belong to him by purchase, pre-emption, or squatter's claim. The territory is supposed to be in some measure governed by the statutes of the State of Oregon, but for every existing law there seems to be another one equally powerful to nullify its effects. For instance, the whole territory is declared to be a prohibition country, and the importation of liquor illegal; if a smuggler is caught red-handed unloading a cargo of whisky he is fined or imprisoned and his cargo confiscated. At the same time there is no law to prevent the sale of liquor within the territory; and when once the cargo is safely run, drinks are sold openly over the bar just as they would be in San Francisco.

The Edmond's Act again sets forth that no white man may live with an Indian woman unless he is married to her, and yet most of the clergy of Alaska refuse to legalise such alliances by the reading of the marriage service.

These two subjects occupy the greater portion of the time devoted to the carrying out of the laws by officials drawing good salaries from the United States government, as long as their own party is in power, but no definite conclusion has ever yet been reached.

Our party consisted of Reed, an English friend, who was going to Cassiar for the big game shooting; Gladman, a Canadian, who had already made two trips to the north in the service of government surveyors, and myself. We had brought with us from Victoria about 1500 lbs. of provisions and ammunition, besides a canoe built of light spruce—in the absence of basswood—on the Peterboro' model, as the most suitable craft for the long journey ahead. Her dimensions were—18 feet length, 3 feet 6 inches beam, and 20 inches depth, with a total weight of 130 lbs. She was subjected to some criticism in Wrangel; and being an innovation on the long-established methods of travel, was at first universally condemned. The fact that she was painted a light blue colour started a suggestion that she was made of zinc, and this opinion took such a firm hold that I found it saved trouble to agree with it and admit that she was made of zinc; but as Reed and Gladman continued to deny the statement, we were looked upon with some mistrust till the dispute was satisfactorily settled.

She proved a lucky boat from the beginning, and maintained her reputation throughout the voyage. As soon as she was finished she was moved from the building shed to more airy quarters to let the paint dry quickly, and the same night the shed, the moulds from which she was built, and a dozen boats and canoes were destroyed by fire. After a journey of 4000 miles of rapid and at times dangerous water; after being carried over long rough portages on men's shoulders, and hauled on dog-sleighs through 200 miles of forest; she reached the salt water again at the end of fifteen months to battle with the storms and tides of the Behring Sea. But she came through it all safe and sound; only once hammer and nails were called into play to patch up a hole made at a simple little rapid on the Dease River, which we ran on the wrong side, through taking the advice of a local man who had just come up stream, and should have been able to give us more correct information about the state of the water.

In comparison with the other types of canoes in common use among the different tribes of natives through whose territory we travelled, and who by long experience have learnt to construct the class of canoe most suited to their home waters, our little ship was inferior in some respect to each of them; but, as a combination of good points, which enabled her to make the whole journey, and come safely through the varied conditions of travel which tested her capabilities to the utmost, I doubt if it would be possible to build a more suitable craft.

The narrow dug-out of the Pacific coast rivers is easy to pole up a rapid current, but her weight forbids any attempt to make a long portage; the birch bark of the Yukon and the northern lakes is light and easily repaired wherever birch trees grow, but she would be shaken to pieces by the rattling of a dog-sleigh through the forest, and would be too frail a vessel to land through the surf of the Behring Sea. The long skin bidarka of the Esquimaux, with her water-tight decks, is the perfection of a sea-going canoe; but she has no room for the stowage of bulky cargo, is uncomfortable to sit in, and hard to navigate round the sharp corners of small streams; while the walrus-skin which covers the light frame is easily torn by collision with a sharp stick which would only scratch a wooden canoe.

The difficulties which we were sure to meet with in the course of transport compelled us to limit our supplies to such things as are strictly indispensable on a long voyage, embracing the varied features of travel by canoe during the season of open water and dog-sleighs when winter set fast the rivers and lakes, through a country not at all well supplied with provisions except such as can be procured by the rifle and fish-nets. The small trading posts on the west side of the mountains are never well stocked with articles that are heavy and expensive to move; the trader makes a much larger profit by importing 100 lbs. weight of blankets or bright-coloured shawls than he could from the same weight of flour or bacon, and the expense of transport is the same in each case. Experience has taught him that, however many boat-loads of provisions are shipped into the interior, they are all consumed without much profit to the importer, who prefers to take the chance of hard times during the winter and the certainty of a larger return for his furs in the spring.

We took with us flour and bacon enough to last for three or four months, tea and tobacco in large quantities, a good supply of ammunition for rifles and shot-guns, nets, hooks, and lines, dog harness, a large canvas lodge similar to the teepee of the Crees and Blackfeet, a Kodak camera, blankets, and a kitchen-box containing kettles, frying-pans, and all such simple necessaries for camp cookery.

There is a small steamer which makes irregular trips on the Stikine during the summer months, taking supplies for the Hudson's Bay Company and the few miners who are still working in Cassiar, as far as the head of navigation at Telegraph Creek; but she had left before our arrival, and would not be sailing again for six weeks. The water in the river was said to be still very high, although the summer floods caused by the melting snow had already begun to subside; and, as it would without doubt prove a difficult task to force our way up stream for 150 miles, we made an attempt to secure an Indian guide to show us the best routes and the shortest cuts, which a stranger may easily miss on such a big river. But the Wrangel Indians have the peculiarities of the race fully developed, and, thinking we could not do without them, were so exorbitant in their demands, and imposed so many conditions, that we soon decided to rely upon our own resources.

A solemn function was the launching of the canoe, and loading her with rather more cargo than she was properly qualified to carry; in fact, we had to leave two or three hundred pounds' weight to come on by a canoe that was expected to start in a few days. Plenty of advice was offered too, and gloomy prophecies of disasters that were likely to happen to such a small craft of a different and therefore presumably inferior model to the recognised type in use on the Stikine, and manned by strangers, who are universally supposed to be incompetent to navigate waters with which they are unfamiliar. A very widely-spread characteristic this of the men who go down to the sea in ships on a small scale. Blue water sailors take a more liberal view, and freely acknowledge a man who takes his vessel in safety across the ocean as their equal in matters nautical, even though he does hail from another port; but the long-shoreman or fisherman of any small harbour will seldom admit that there may be men, less lucky in the matter of their birthplace, who can handle a boat as well as a native of their own particular mud-hole.

I hope nobody counted the number of drinks of illicit whisky we finished on that sunny afternoon in Wrangel. Several times we were just starting when some hospitable miner would insist on our coming back for just one more farewell drink, and we trooped back along the little street to the grog-shop for another gulp. Luckily it was quite calm, and the heavy load at the bottom of the canoe kept us fairly steady till the labour of paddling against a strong tide gradually toned down our hilarity. For the first mile we hugged the rocky shore of Wrangel Island till we reached its northern end, and then stood away for the mainland to take advantage of any slack water there might be to work our way against the freshet that was pouring out of the river. There were several high bluffs to be rounded where we could use neither line nor poles; the current ran with the force of a rapid, and two or three attempts were often necessary before we could struggle round with the paddles. It was ten o'clock, but still good daylight, when we passed Rothsay Point, and camped fairly within the mouth of the river. From this camp we had our last view of the salt water for many a long day; a grand scene, with the after-glow of a northern sunset resting on snowfield and glacier, and the black points of the countless pine trees outlined sharply against the western sky. Mainland and islands were confused by the elaborate windings of the coast-line; deep gloomy inlets ran far inland under the shadow of the high mountains, and the network of channels leading in every direction through the archipelago lay like streaks of oil undisturbed by the slightest ripple, and reflecting faithfully the wonders of the sky above. A great silence reigned over everything, broken only by the splash of a salmon or the cry of a loon or gull, and even on this bright summer evening one could feel the ever-present sense of gloom which the vast and inaccessible in nature always produce. Can these frowning peaks and dense pine forests which almost defy exploration, lying in a land of almost perpetual rain and snow, ever become of use for maintaining a civilised portion of the human race? The same question, with the exception of a rather better climate, was applicable fifty years ago to the coasts of Oregon, Washington, and British Columbia, yet these countries now support a small but fairly prosperous population, and there seems to be a good chance for Southern Alaska to occupy the same position as her resources are developed. The establishment of salmon canneries has already met with success; the export of timber must shortly be legalised; and surely some few valuable quartz ledges exist among those vast mountain ranges which guard their secrets so well, and afford so sure a sanctuary to the mountain goat, the bear, the marmot, and the ptarmigan.

The scarcity of dry firewood, owing to the heavy rainfall, is one of the greatest drawbacks to travelling on the lower Stikine. The valley back from the river is covered with an almost impenetrable growth of pine timber, rank underbrush, and steaming moss, while the "Devil's Club"—a long cane-like stalk covered with thorns, bearing a crown of leaves furnished in the same manner—lies in ambush till the weight of a man's foot causes it to start up and strike the intruder in the face. This forest, favoured by the warmth and moisture of the ocean, runs far up the mountain sides, till it meets the snow that for ever covers the peaks of the coast range on either side of the river. The scenery much resembles that of the Fraser where it passes through the same range, except that on the Stikine River the mountains are higher and more rugged, and glaciers, sometimes coming right down into the river valley, are of frequent occurrence. The source of the Stikine has never been exactly defined, but its tributaries are known to head with those of the Peace and Liard, on the unexplored Pacific Arctic watershed lying between the 56th and 58th parallels of north latitude.

The difficulty of ascending this river in flood time will be at once understood when I say that we were unable to make headway with the paddles against the current, in mid-stream, at any point in the journey of 150 miles; so that we had always to creep along the bank that seemed most likely to offer slack water. The straight side of any reach is usually the best, as the current naturally sweeps into the curves with the greatest force. There was no beach along which a line might be used, as the river was up to the level of the forest growth, and in many places the banks had caved in; or a huge pine had dropped into the stream, and a detour into the strength of the current, or a crossing to the far shore, which entailed a loss of a couple of hundred yards, was necessary. Great caution had to be used in rounding these obstructions, to make sure that we could hold our own with the current before edging back for the shelter of the bank—to be swept under a fallen tree meant a certain capsize, probably with disastrous results. No bottom could be reached with the poles, but we had often a chance to pull over a stretch of bad water by laying hold of overhanging bushes. When no other plan was practicable, a man would go ahead through the woods with a coil of line, and making one end fast to a log, throw it out clear of the bank. When the log came bobbing down to the canoe it was seized; the other end of the line was made fast to a tree, and the canoe hauled up hand over hand. This manœuvre generally occupied a good deal of time, as the line often fouled a bush or sunken crag, and was sometimes very difficult to clear. In other places the river was split up by islands into several channels, and, having no pilot, we were obliged to use our own judgment in making a choice of routes. Sometimes we paddled up a long winding backwater—the slough of the American, the *ch'naï* of the French-Canadian—only to find its head blocked by immense piles of drift timber, over which we had to make a difficult portage, or run back and try another channel. At the head of each island there was usually a submerged gravel bar and a swift current with a slight overfall; and here it was necessary to get out and wade with the canoe up stream, to clear the bar before crossing to slacker water.

The general direction of the river is to the eastward for the first 20 miles, but from the "big bend" of the miners it turns directly to the north for 65 miles, afterwards bending to the north-east, and continuing on this course beyond Telegraph Creek. Of the many tributaries that enter the lower river, the most important is the Iskoot, coming in from the eastward about 30 miles from the mouth of the Stikine, and bending back nearly parallel to this stream. A party of four miners ascended the Iskoot in the spring and summer of 1891, leaving Wrangel with hand-sleighs, and building a boat on the breaking up of the ice. Although gold was found in many places, it was always in small quantities, and no paying bars were discovered. The river is full of obstructions to navigation, and consequently difficult to travel on; but these miners succeeded in forcing their way to the north-east for a considerable distance, and eventually crossed overland to Telegraph Creek, in the autumn. They reported game to be abundant; black and grizzly bear were numerous along the river, especially during the salmon run, and goats were sighted nearly every day. In fact, the mountain goat is very common throughout the whole length of the coast range, from the Fraser northwards. One of the most stupid of American animals, it owes its safety to the inaccessibility of its haunts, for it is no small undertaking to leave the river or salt water and climb 5000 feet of steep mountain side, clothed for three-quarters of the distance with a dense pine growth starting out of the accumulated forest débris of centuries, and only giving place at last to granite walls and drifts of everlasting snow. The results of one of these expeditions is usually pleasing enough—you can kill the goats without any further trouble; you can watch the strange little marmots which have their homes in the rocks, and throw stones at the ptarmigan which will hardly move out of your way. If the day happens to be clear, you will have a view of mountain peaks and forests, unnamed and untraversed, that it is useless to attempt to depict; and, when the sun goes down, you may build your fire in a sheltered gulch, eat roasted goat-flesh, and spend a night among the grandest works of nature. But it seems unpractical. The hardest labour of all is to carry a load of meat down to the camp; and the wily Indian asks himself why he should go to so much trouble when he can load his canoe with salmon in a couple of hours, or perhaps kill a fat bear close to the river, and pass the rest of the day lying on his back in the enjoyment of his pipe and such easy thoughts as present themselves to his untroubled mind. So the goats are not much molested, and many of them live out their pleasant existence without ever crossing the path of the hated human being.

CHAPTER II

ON THE STIKINE RIVER

The Stikine glacier—Overtaken by coast Indians—Canoe drill at Little Cañon—Difference in climate on opposite sides of coast range—Salmon catching—Habits of bears—Klootchman Cañon—The Chinook jargon—Telegraph Creek—Freight charges.

FOR the first few days after leaving Wrangel we had wonderfully fine weather, and in spite of all difficulties made fair progress by poling, paddling, wading, and pulling ourselves up by the bushes, till we reached the great glacier—by far the most striking of all—the Stikine glacier. It issues from a low pass in the mountains on the west side and comes right down into the valley, broadening out as it reaches the low ground, and presenting a base three miles in length towards the river, at no great distance from the bank. It would well repay any one to spend a week or two in thoroughly exploring the sources of this vast ice-field, especially as it is so easily reached by water, and no hard

ON THE STIKINE RIVER.

climbing is necessary. Great caution should be used though, as the only attempt that seems to have been made to explore this glacier was attended with most lamentable results. Before the sale of Alaska to the Americans, a Russian man-of-war once sent a boat's crew up the Stikine to examine the river as far as possible, and to report on its practicability for commerce. On arriving at the great glacier the officers in charge of the expedition set out to explore the ice-field and were never again heard of. A long search was made for them, but their bodies were not found, and no doubt they met their death by falling into a crevasse.

According to some of the miners who remember the Stikine twenty years ago, the glacier is receding from the river; and the Indians have a legend to the effect that it once extended right across the Stikine, and the water found its way through a tunnel under the ice. The only fact that might give a slight aspect of truth to the story is the existence of a little ice-field high up the mountain side across the river, just opposite the great glacier.

And now the clouds came rolling up from the ocean, the mountains were hidden, a gray curtain hung over the valley, and day after day the rain poured down in an almost continual stream. The river, too, was more difficult, being broken up by islands and gravel bars into numerous winding channels, all more or less blocked by snags and drift piles. We kept on travelling a few hours at a time, and every night found us a little farther ahead. It was useless to wait, as this sort of weather is known to last a month at a time on the lower Stikine, and there seemed no reason why the clouds should not remain penned between the high mountains and the downpour continue for ever.

It was not an easy matter to find good camping places, for dry wood was scarce and not always convenient to a landing where the cargo could be unloaded and the canoe hauled up. This has to be done every night during high water, on account of the uprooted trees and masses of drift logs that are continually floating down stream to the great peril of any boat left moored to the bank for a night. The canvas lodge stretched over four or five leaning poles under the spreading limbs of a big spruce tree gave us shelter enough, but our camp fires were seldom satisfactory, and clothes and blankets when once wet, had to remain wet till the sun should shine again. The mosquitoes were another source of annoyance, but they were not nearly as bad as we had been led to expect by the terrible accounts we had heard of them at Fort Wrangel.

During this time we were overtaken by a large salt-water canoe manned by a crew of coast Indians, who were on their way to the dry country lying to the eastward of the mountains, with the intention of salmon fishing and berry picking. The Wrangel Indians are well provided with all the necessaries of life in their own country—salmon and a large variety of sea fish are to be caught in abundance, wildfowl are fairly plentiful, and the islands are wonderfully well stocked with the Alaskan variety of the little Virginian deer, and black bear; but the rain is so persistent that the curing of fish or meat by drying over the smoke of a camp fire is almost an impossibility. So the coast Indians make yearly expeditions to the upper waters of the Stikine, where the climate is much better, and the salmon are more easily caught than in the salt water. On these occasions they generally bring up a small stock of trading goods to barter with the interior tribes for moose-skin and other commodities not procurable on the coast.

These Indians who now caught us up had left Wrangel two days after us, and had been lucky enough to get a strong fair wind which enabled them to run the first 40 miles under canvas without trouble. They had with them a white man, one of the pioneers of the Cassiar diggings, who, after seventeen years absence was now going back to examine a quartz ledge which he had discovered in early days. These tricks of memory, which exaggerate a trace of mineral in a mountain of rock into a valuable deposit of the precious metals, are a great source of consolation to the miner; and a man must be wretched indeed who has not some dim vision of a rich quartz ledge discovered years ago to cheer him up under the many disappointments to which the life of a placer miner is subject. The ledge is usually situated in an inaccessible country as far as possible from the discoverer's present position; it was hit upon by chance, at a time when the approach of winter and general misery made it impossible to thoroughly examine the richness of the find. But if an expedition is fitted out to search for it again, the miner usually proves an incompetent pilot, or the ledge turns out as worthless as the thousands of other ledges which have held so much promise for the sanguine discoverer.

We travelled in company with the other canoe, both crews taking things easily till we reached the Little Cañon, 75 miles from the mouth of the river.

The Little Cañon, so called to distinguish it from the Great Cañon above Telegraph Creek, is the only real obstruction on the navigable part of the stream. During certain stages of water it is impassable for anything but a powerful steamer, and she must be carefully handled in the whirlpools to avoid collision with the cliffs on either side. When we arrived there, the water had fallen several feet from its highest summer level; but the first glance showed us that it was doubtful whether we could get through in safety, even with the double crews—for it was obvious that white men and Indians were now on level terms, and must help each other, or wait for a week or two at the foot of the cañon for the water to fall. We might, indeed, have portaged our little canoe by chopping out a trail a mile in length over a rough hill covered with burnt timber, but it would have been no light work. Professor Dawson describes this cañon as being "three-fifths of a mile in length, and in places not more than 50 yards wide, bordered by massive granite cliffs 200 to 300 feet in height." Through this narrow gorge the whole volume of the Stikine waters rushes in wild swirls, while ragged points abutting from the bluffs create strong eddies to add to the confusion of water. The worst whirlpools are at the lower entrance, one on each side, at the meeting of the main current with the eddies that rush round the bays below the first points of the cañon. We camped on the east bank, on the spot where many a Cassiar miner has waited for the water to go down, and passed four days in vain attempts to overcome the obstacle ahead. Our first trial was a most senseless affair, but the steersman of the big canoe had great faith in it. So we discharged half the cargo from his vessel, boomed out a huge sprit-sail on each side, and holding our paddles in readiness, boldly attempted to sail through everything in front of a strong fair wind. The long canoe simply flew up the eddy; but on striking the current, we were helpless. Nine men working with oars and paddles made no impression, and the next minute the bow swung off, the sails gybed, and the whirlpool taking charge, carried us back to the quiet water below. This programme was gone through several times, and always with the same result, till at last our steersman lost his enthusiasm and gave up the attempt for the day.

The following morning we went to work in a more methodical manner, and, putting ashore at the first point, passed a long line to the top of the cliff. Three men were left in the canoe and the rest of us scrambled up, and, clearing the line from overhanging rocks and trees to its full length, hauled the canoe bodily over the steep overfall at the point. About a quarter of a mile was gained in this manner, but then we were obliged to cross and try to reach an eddy on the far side. We shoved off from the rocks with as much headway as possible, but before we were half-way across, it was clear that we should miss the eddy. A timely order in English to "back water" saved us from being carried on to a jagged point, and in a couple of minutes we were opposite the camp that we had left three hours before. Every morning and afternoon, the Indian Captain Tomyot turned us out for this canoe drill; but although we nearly got through several times, a piece of wild steering, or the breaking of a line or pole, always spoilt the result of many hours' work.

Among the native crew was a fellow who presented a typical combination of all the bad points in the Indian character, fully developed by a slight leaven of education and a remarkable aptitude for picking up the vices of the white man. Some years ago, in a drunken scuffle on an outlying island on the coast, he had bitten off a woman's ear, and after losing his nose in the same manner by way of retaliation, had been taken in charge by the U.S. authorities. He was sentenced to three years in a San Francisco gaol, but appears to have enjoyed rather an easy life of it while working out his time. Some benevolent person took him in hand, taught him to read and write, and made him a model redman generally. On his return to Alaska, he was welcomed back by his people as a distinguished traveller and a man who had seen something of the world, and has since been looked upon with great respect. He is cunning enough to make the most of this and turn it to his own advantage; but, at the same time, he is doing a great deal of harm among the Wrangel Indians—his little knowledge suggesting plans for ill deeds that would not be likely to occur to his more simple-minded companions.

This man, when he was in the right humour, was as good a bowsman as could be found anywhere; but he had little inclination for a long struggle with the strong water of the cañon, and usually stayed in camp with the women while we were making our various attempts.

On the fifth morning there were great preparations, and the Indians painted their faces to ensure success. The noseless man meant business too, and his countenance was more repulsive than ever in the glory of a coat of scarlet. The others all preferred stripes of red and black, while the women went in for solid black, although they had no intention of risking their babies in tiny baskets in the whirlpools of the cañon. Old Tomyot, the steersman, told us we were sure to get through now, and drew our attention to the fact that the water had fallen several inches, which would no doubt help the powers of the paint.

By this time we were pretty well perfect in our drill. We knew all the rocks and stumps on the summit of the cliffs that were likely to foul the line; we knew the submerged ledges where the poles would reach bottom, and the cracks in the granite where the men in the bow could get a grip with their iron boathooks. Experience had taught us where we could cross the current, where the eddies could be worked, and where we could climb up and down the bluffs in safety. Everything went well; not a mistake was made, and, late in the afternoon, we hauled clear of the cañon, passed into comparatively quiet water above, and landed our cargo. This had occupied over six hours; and now, drifting down with the stream, and only paddling enough to keep clear of rocks, we reached the camp in eight minutes. The next day we brought up the rest of the cargo, and the small canoe at the same time, the women making an overland portage.

The Little Cañon is the gate into an entirely different country from that which we had passed through on the lower river. The coast range lay behind us, and the distorted peaks and glacier-covered gulches had given way to gently rounded summits of much less elevation, with very little snow upon them, and lying further back from the river. On the east side of the mountains there is every indication of a great change in the climate. Dry benches well covered with grass and berry bushes show up, small birch trees are numerous, and much of the country has been burnt—affording a strong contrast to the dank forest below, where no fire could ever hold its own.

This difference in climate on the opposite sides of the coast range is only a continuation of what may be observed under the same conditions in British Columbia, Washington, and Oregon, which all show sharply defined belts of wet and dry climates; but here perhaps it is more strongly marked owing to the extraordinary depth of rain and snowfall which prevails from Wrangel to the Little Cañon, where the snow lies ten feet deep through the winter, while 50 miles further up stream there is rarely more than two feet on the level. At Wrangel, potatoes frequently rot in the ground when irrigation is necessary to ensure a crop at Telegraph Creek.

Of the berries—the raspberry, the soap berry, and the saskatoon, service, or bear-berry, as it is called in different parts of the west—are most plentiful. The soap berry is a small red fruit with rather an unpleasant bitter taste, but it is a great favourite among the Indians. They gather a large kettleful of these berries and pound them up with their hands till a thick froth, much resembling soap bubbles, gathers on the top of the kettle. This froth, with a judicious mixture of salmon oil—or, better still, seal oil—they consider one of the things worth living for.

All the little streams were full of salmon, for the run was now at its height, and vast quantities of fish were crowding up as far as the water would carry them. Our Indian friends were reaping a rich harvest. A long stick with an iron hook lashed on the end is the only outfit required. The fisherman takes up a position on a rock below a little rapid where the salmon are likely to lie to gather strength for a rush, and gently feels the water down-stream with the butt of his pole. Presently he touches a fish; the pole is quickly reversed, and a sharp stroke across the current lands the victim on the bank. As soon as the fish are caught they are handed over to the women, who, as is usual with Indians, get none of the sport and have all the dirty work to do. The salmon are cleaned, split open for the purpose of removing the backbone, and laid on large scaffolds built in a sunny spot; smouldering fires of bark are lit underneath, and constant attention is necessary to turn the fish at the right time, so that sun and smoke may do an equal share of the drying. The winter's supply is put up during the two or three weeks of the big run. The incredible numbers of salmon that swarm in the rivers of the Pacific have been written about so exhaustively that it is unnecessary to say much upon the subject. The Stikine as yet shows no diminution in the quantity of its fish, as there are no canneries to thin them out as has so obviously been the case on the Columbia, and in a less marked degree on the Fraser, the Skeena, and the Naas. Ugly brutes these salmon are, so far away from salt water, with their red bellies, slimy green backs, and threadbare fins; but nevertheless they form the staple article of food for the native population. Along the salmon streams and in the berry patches the tracks of bear were plentiful, but at this time of year, when they are feeding entirely on fish, their flesh is hardly edible, and of course the fur is in poor condition, so we never hunted for them and did not happen to see any along the river; but in the late autumn or early spring the whole valley of the Stikine, from the sea upwards, would no doubt be a good hunting ground for both black bear and the so-called grizzly.

The extreme variation in the skins of the grizzlies that are killed on the Stikine gives ample scope for argument on the long discussed and so far undecided question as to how many different kinds of bear exist in North America. Black, brown, grizzly, cinnamon, silver-tipped, and bald-face—are they all varieties of one species, or, as some say, of two? or do they represent six distinct animals? I have known great authorities on the subject of bears completely at a loss to name some small skins of evidently full-grown bears, almost as white as the skin of a polar, and known to the Indians as the white rock bear, which are occasionally brought in from the high peaks of the coast range bordering the valleys of the Skeena and Naas.

Dirty feeders are bears of all kinds in the salmon time; and when their first hunger is satiated they are very particular in picking out the most repulsive form of dirtiness. In the little rapids they can always snatch out a live fish without trouble, but they greatly prefer the dead ones stranded by the fallen water. I have often watched them on summer evenings, just after sundown, nosing over the carcasses rotting on a gravel bar till they find one sufficiently putrid to suit them, and then spending several minutes in licking the stones for the last flavour of the delicate morsel.

Canoe-travelling above the Little Cañon was much more enjoyable than in the lower reaches. In addition to fine weather, we were often favoured with a strong fair wind, when a small piece of canvas or a blanket set as a squaresail pulled us over strong water that we could not have stemmed with poles or paddles. It was rather dangerous sailing though, as the squalls were sometimes fierce and variable under the high land; and we had to keep a close watch on the halyards in order to lower the sail at once in case of being caught aback. The temptation is, of course, to carry on too long when you find you are making good headway against a strong current without doing any work; and a canoe has a tendency to bury her nose and fill up very suddenly under a pressure of canvas. One more cañon had to be passed, but here there was no difficulty; indeed, it is known, in derision, as the Klootchman Cañon—"Klootchman" being the name for woman in the Chinook jargon universally employed between whites and Indians on the Pacific coast. Here it has always been the custom for the men to lay down their paddles and let the women take complete charge of the navigation, and very competent they are to do so, except in high water, when the current sweeps strongly round the upper points, and sometimes the task proves too much for their strength. There are stories of canoes lying at this cañon for days because the women were short of power and the men would not put hand to pole or paddle.

The Chinook jargon, invented long ago by a French fur trader on the Columbia for his own convenience in bartering with local Indians, has spread all along the northern Pacific coast and far into the interior wherever the miners have penetrated. From its original use between whites and Indians, it has developed into a common language between the various tribes whose native tongues are totally distinct within very short distances. It is freely used too by the Chinese, and, in fact, by people of all nationalities who cannot speak English. Chinook is easily picked up, as it is composed of very few words, and most of them French or English. The absence of all grammatical rules tends to make one's meaning a little doubtful at times, but it is a distinct advance on the old sign language, which causes so many complications in dealing with natives.

The current above the Klootchman Cañon was swift, but there were few islands or outlying bars; and by frequent crossings we could generally make use of slack water under one bank. On the 1st of August we reached Glenora, or, as it is more generally called, "Steamboat Landing," a long row of deserted log cabins, prettily situated under a high cliff on the west side of the river. In the old mining days it was a place of some importance; and the cabins will no doubt be all occupied again during the next "strike" in Cassiar, which is so anxiously expected by the ever-sanguine miners. At present the only permanent resident is the customs-house officer, who keeps a jealous eye on everything coming up the river, notwithstanding the fact that he is a hundred miles inside the British line. He was very good to us though, and, as we heard that the pack train from Telegraph Creek to Dease Lake had already left, we stayed at Glenora for a couple of days' rest.

There is probably no harder manual labour than

that of driving a heavily-loaded canoe up a rapid river, especially for the steersman, who, besides the constant paddling, has an extra strain on his wrists in keeping the bow from sheering while winding in and out of the little bays to take advantage of the slack water close to the bank.

Above Glenora the river becomes narrow, and the pace of the current increases to a strength of eight knots in mid-stream. There are several small rapids, too, which require some care to pass in safety. The worst of these, a mile or so above Glenora, is a treacherous piece of water, and has claimed several victims, white and Indian. On a second journey up the Stikine, I was nearly a witness of one of these accidents. We had just hauled through the rapid with a sea-going canoe, and were boiling a kettle on a gravel bar round the next bend, when another canoe came down stream manned by three white men and an Indian steersman. They put ashore and spent half an hour with us, as we were bringing up all the late news from the outside world and had some letters for them. Five minutes after they left us their canoe capsized in the rapid and two of the occupants were drowned, yet the place looks easy enough to run,

THE GLENORA RAPID.

and their canoe was a big powerful craft piloted by an Indian well known as a competent steersman.

Four miles below Telegraph Creek is Buck's Bar, the place where gold was first discovered in any quantity on the Stikine, and lately celebrated as the scene of one of those misguided mining enterprises that have done a great deal to prevent the development of British Columbian gold-fields. So many companies have been formed and so much capital expended for the extraction of gold from far-off places where no large amount of gold ever existed, that the long-suffering public have at last become chary of purchasing shares. Several of the placer camps, notably Cariboo, were extremely rich as long as they lasted; but so far it is hard to name any single quartz ledge or deposit of auriferous gravel suitable for the hydraulic method of washing that has ever paid a single dollar to the shareholders. Yet just across the international boundary line, to the southward of British Columbia, in a country of the same geological formation, and presenting the same obstacles to exploration and the transport of machinery, quartz ledges have long been worked to advantage; and it seems hardly probable that the 49th parallel of latitude should form the line of demarcation between the natural resources of the earth as well as between its inhabitants.

Telegraph Creek received its name in anticipation that was never realised; for here the electric wire intended to connect the Old World and the New, by way of Behring Straits, was to cross the Stikine. For the two years, '66, '67, parties of energetic explorers followed up unknown mountain passes, and cut supply trails through the thickly-wooded interior of British Columbia and Alaska, in search of the most feasible route for a telegraph line, only to be met on their return with the news that the Atlantic cable—which had been pronounced an impossibility—was in full working order, and that the overland scheme was in consequence abandoned. The creek itself is very small; although it has been found to yield gold, as is the case with most of the tributaries of the Stikine, the results have always been unsatisfactory.

A few miles higher up the main stream is the foot of the Grand Cañon of the Stikine, the beginning of a long stretch of unnavigable water. The Indians make use of the river again above the cañon, but I could get no definite information as to how far they have ascended towards its source.

The little town of Telegraph stands at the junction of the creek with the river, deep down in a narrow valley, shut in by high mountains over which the sun never rises in the short days of winter; but it has rather more life than Glenora, being the starting-point for the pack train that carries all necessaries for the scattered population of Cassiar to the head of Dease Lake. It is also rather an important centre for the fur trade, as there are two or three rival stores, and a keen competition has arisen. The Indian has soon learnt to appreciate the advantages of competition, and prices have gone up to such an extent that one would suppose fur was hardly worth buying at such figures. Besides the inhabitants of the large villages of Tahl-Tan, situated 12 miles higher up the river, and the hunters from the large tract of country lying towards the Taku River and Teslin Lake to the westward of the Stikine, a band of Indians known as the "Bear Lakes," bring their furs overland for several hundred miles from the head-waters of the Peace River, to take advantage of the high prices offered by the opposing traders. There is certainly no other trading post in the whole of Canada that takes in as many silver foxes as are annually traded at Telegraph Creek, and good skins too, many of them fetching a price in a Regent Street furrier's shop that might form a vast subject for the wretched, cold-fingered Indian to ponder on as he sets his line of steel traps where the snow has drifted hard on the bleak slopes of the open mountains over which the foxes roam throughout the long northern winter. Next in order of numbers are the bear skins, but these are for the most part killed along the Stikine, as the hides are too heavy to carry long distances. Wolf, lynx, beaver, marten, and wolverines, in smaller quantities, swell the yearly fur trade at Telegraph to a very respectable total.

We had expected some trouble in getting our canoe carried over the seventy mile portage to the lake, and were prepared to do it ourselves if necessary, but a couple of Indians undertook the work readily enough, and fulfilled their agreement in a most satisfactory manner.

After a week's delay the mule train came in, and the following morning we started with our cargo distributed on the backs of five animals. A charge of seven cents a pound is now made on all freight carried over the portage, a great falling off, from the packer's point of view, since the first pack train went into Cassiar with a load of 15,000 lbs. at fifty cents a pound, and cleared a fortune for the owners before competition cut the business down. There is still enough work to keep a train busy during the summer months, as this route is the only inlet into an immense territory inhabited by Indians who have acquired many of the white man's habits, and clamour for things they would never have known the names of if Cassiar had remained purely a fur-trading district, but which have become necessaries for the natives since the influx of the miners.

CHAPTER III

THE DISTRICT OF CASSIAR

Cassiar trail—Laketon—A Hudson Bay trading post—Dease Lake—Drawbacks to mining—Sylvester's Landing—Casca Indians—Abandon plan of wintering on Frances Lake.

THE Cassiar trail was once a well-travelled route, with stopping-places every few miles where meals and fiery whisky — specially prepared for use in mining camps—could be bought at high figures. But these signs of prosperity have fallen into decay, and the rough log cabins are unoccupied. The trails and bridges are, however, kept in good order by the British Columbian Government. The portage to the Arctic slope is a remarkably easy one, without any noticeable height of land; while the only difficult parts of the trail are the steep hills at the crossings of two large tributaries of the Stikine, known as the First and Second North Fork, which run through deep cañons that seem a conspicuous feature of all these streams. Near the First North Fork, 12 miles from Telegraph Creek, the trail runs through Tahl-Tan, but it was entirely deserted when we passed, as the inhabitants were making the most of the salmon run to put up their winter supply of dried fish. For a great part of the distance to the lake the trail lies along dry open benches, afterwards changing to spruce and poplar-covered flats, with many swampy spots. The general appearance of the mountains that are occasionally seen is very pleasing to the sportsman's eye. The summits are rounded, and on the sides are large stretches of open grassland, interspersed with patches of light timber. Many of these mountains are well known to the Indians as a sure find for cariboo and mountain sheep; while the moose, which of late years have pushed their way to the westward, are rapidly increasing in number in the more level country, and have even been killed within a few miles of Telegraph Creek.

The pack train was composed of thirty-five heavily loaded mules, which were, of course, driven at a slow pace, so that 15 miles were considered a good day's travel. Early starts were made to avoid the heat of the sun and give the animals time to feed and rest in the afternoon. The loads should be off and the day's work over not later than eleven o'clock, if mules or horses are to be kept in good condition and packed regularly for any length of time.

On the morning of 16th August we crossed the slight elevation marking the watershed between the streams running into the Pacific and Arctic Oceans; and shortly afterwards reached the head of Dease Lake — a narrow sheet of water running some 24 miles directly northwards, with thickly-wooded shores gently sloping upwards to the summits of low hills, and here and there a towering snow-capped peak standing well back from the water.

A dilapidated little steamer still plies on the lake; and putting the canoe on deck, we took passage by her to Laketon, the most important town in Cassiar, situated at the mouth of Dease Creek, 18 miles down on the west side of the lake, where we were royally entertained for the night by Mr. Porter, the Gold Commissioner for the district.

Laketon is a good specimen of the deserted mining town so frequently seen to the westward of the Rocky Mountains. Dease Creek was one

DINNER CAMP *EN ROUTE.*

of the richest strikes; and in 1874-75 several hundred miners, with their parasites the storekeepers and bar-tenders, made the camp lively. Gold dust was flying about with the recklessness distinctive of the life; but now the young shoots of the forest are pushing up in the streets, and rows of empty houses stare out across the lake, apparently brooding over old scenes of good times and debauchery—better, perhaps, undescribed—that were enacted within their walls.

In 1834 Mr. J. M'Leod, a chief trader in the Hudson's Bay Company's service, acting under the instructions of the Governor, left Fort Simpson on the Mackenzie and ascended the Liard to explore its upper waters—hoping, if possible, to cross the watershed and find some stream running to the Pacific,—with the view of controlling the western fur trade, which was then in dispute between the Russians and the Company. In this undertaking he was successful; and, turning up Dease River at its junction with the Liard, eventually reached the Stikine, passing through Dease Lake, which he named after the Arctic explorer. It was not, however, until four years later that Mr. Robert Campbell established a trading post on the lake, where he passed a winter of unusual hardship from starvation. He mentions in his report that at one time his party were obliged to eat their parchment windows and the lacing of their snowshoes, besides being in danger from the coast Indians, who seem to have had a bad reputation at that time. The post was abandoned in May 1839, as the trouble about the trading rights at the mouth of the Stikine had been amicably settled by the leasing of the long narrow coast strip of Alaska to the Company. The whole trade was thus controlled without the difficulty and expense of maintaining a post on Dease Lake. For more than thirty years the Cassiar District was left as M'Leod found it, for Campbell, one of the most enthusiastic and successful explorers that ever entered the Hudson's Bay Company's service, was turning his attention to a more northern country, and making fresh discoveries in the direction of Frances Lake and the upper waters of what is now known as the Yukon River.

In 1872 Messrs. M'Culloch and Thibert, after a three years' prospecting expedition, reached Dease Lake by the same route that M'Leod and Campbell had travelled over, after having discovered gold near the site of old Fort Halkett on the Liard. Their intention was to winter on the lake, trusting to their rifles and what fish they might catch for their supplies; but they were told by the Indians that gold had been discovered on the Stikine, and that white men were already working there. So they crossed over the divide and found the mining camp at Buck's Bar. In the spring they started back for Fort Halkett, but finding a much better prospect on Thibert's Creek—a small stream coming in from the west near the foot of Dease Lake,— they worked there with success. Other miners soon followed them from the Stikine, and glowing accounts of the new fields that reached the outside world caused a rush from the nearly worked out diggings of Cariboo and Omineca. Thibert is still mining and prospecting in the country (we afterwards met him on Dease River), but M'Culloch was frozen to death near the mouth of the Stikine at the beginning of the Cassiar excitement.

For a couple of years the camp paid well; but then the output of gold decreased, and has continued steadily to do so, till at the present day there are not more than twenty white miners in the whole district, and I doubt if many of these are working paying claims—hanging on year after year in the hope of better times coming on the discovery of a new strike. A few Chinamen make up the mining population, being of a persevering nature, satisfied with small returns for their labour, and extremely reticent as to the amount of gold they have taken out.

A good deal of prospecting was done in early days; and most of the creeks tributary to the Dease and Liard have been worked; but only three of them seem to have been very remunerative—Dease and Thibert's Creek already mentioned, and MacDame's Creek entering the Dease River from the west side, about 60 miles below the outlet of the lake.

The great drawbacks to the country are the shortness of the season during which mining is possible, and the high price of provisions caused by the long and expensive transport by steamer and pack train from Fort Wrangel. Even now that the excitement is over and prices have been cut down as much as possible to suit the hard times, a 100 lb. sack of flour costs 14 dollars at

Dease Lake and £20 on the Liard; bacon 35 to 50 cents a pound; and everything else in proportion. Even the meat and fish supply brought in by the Indians fetches the absurdly high figures which were willingly paid in early days, and the hunters can make a living so easily that they simply refuse to hunt meat if any attempt is made to cut down prices. But if a white man is any use at all in the woods, he ought to be able to keep himself in meat, as there are plenty of cariboo on the bare mountains on the east side of the lake, and the moose are increasing in numbers every year on the lower ground. There are but few miners who can afford to prospect under the present conditions, as, even if paying diggings are discovered, the first year's work is lost, and a capital of several hundred dollars is necessary to buy provisions for a winter's inactivity, to say nothing of the only too probable chance of disappointment and hard work thrown away — for hard work there is sure to be on foot or afloat in any attempt to penetrate far into this little-known corner of British Columbia and the North-West Territories.

We left the lake in company with an Indian

who was bound down stream in his canoe; and travelled in a generally northerly direction down the rapid tortuous course of the Dease River, which is a small stream at the outlet of the lake, but rapidly increases in size by the inflow of water from other creeks. A few miles down stream are some sharp curves, and a little care is required to keep a boat from fouling the drift piles which lie in the full sweep of the current; but otherwise there is no danger to be met with. Four small lakes lie in the course of the river, the longest perhaps two miles in length—very pretty sheets of water with densely-wooded shores and high bald mountains in the background. These lakes are, however, a serious impediment to the navigation of the Dease, as they freeze up much earlier in the autumn than the river, and are often impassable by the middle of October, except to a light boat that can be easily hauled over the ice.

Thirty miles below Dease Lake is the Cottonwood Rapid, but it is easily run, as the few rocks in mid-stream are seen at a glance, and the waves at the foot of the rapids are small on the east side.

On 19th August, early in the morning, we

reached Sylvester's Landing at the mouth of MacDame's Creek, the headquarters of the Hudson's Bay Company's district of Cassiar. A casual glance at once shows the contrast in the appearance of this western trading post as compared with any of the Company's establishments in the same latitude on the eastern side of the Rockies. The slovenly log buildings, the row of Indian shanties in close proximity to the master's house, and the absence of any attempt at regularity in the positions of the various storehouses, compare unfavourably with the neatly kept forts on the northern lakes, where the Hudson's Bay Company has held undisputed sway for a century. It is evident that the strict regime instituted in the time of Prince Rupert has been rudely ended by the appearance of the miner; and the Indian has lost his respect for the white man. He refuses any longer to trade on the "Pro pelle cutem" system of the Hudson's Bay Company, and at the same time has picked up many other habits of civilisation far less to his own advantage.

The remnants of the once numerous tribe of Casca Indians present a good example of the rapid deterioration of natives, caused by free intercourse with the whites—especially, perhaps, with a class of whites which is always to be found in the mining camps. It is only a quickly told chapter in the story that was begun 400 years ago on the Atlantic seaboard—the story of the red man giving way to the white, and sinking through the various stages of disease and degradation into total extinction. What other fate can be in store for a native race when the hunters leave the woods to work for wages and drink the forbidden fire-water, while the women live in luxury on the proceeds of their immorality? No pious missionary has ever penetrated into Cassiar to point out these matters to the Indians, although the district is easily reached, and there is certainly a most hopeful band of sinners, white and Indian, waiting to be converted. Perhaps it is too late to begin, as, at the present rate of mortality, the Cascas will be extinct in ten years' time, and the banks of the Dease and Liard depopulated, unless minerals of sufficient value are discovered to induce the miners to permanently occupy the place of the natives they have so quickly exterminated. Apart from the minerals, the country is absolutely worthless; the soil is usually poor and thickly covered with trees, burnt in many places, and of no commercial value on account of their distance from market; these alternate with swamps and rocky lakes. Even where the land would repay cultivation, the long winters and late summer frosts are serious obstacles to agriculture.

The immediate neighbourhood of Sylvester's Landing is especially favoured in this respect, having a milder climate and producing better crops of hardy vegetables than any other part of the district; in fact, when the diggings on MacDame's Creek were prosperous, a large amount of garden produce was grown for the use of the camp, and potatoes are still raised in some quantity by the Chinese, who are mining 12 miles up the creek at China Bar. A couple of miles further on is a collection of log cabins locally known as "town," where a store is kept up for supplying the wants of the few miners who are still working on the creek. Provisions are boated down from Dease Lake to Sylvester's Landing, and packed from there with horses along a good trail following the valley of MacDame's Creek. Fourteen miles again above the town is Quartz Creek, a tributary of MacDame's, where gold is being taken out in some quantity by two of the most enterprising miners in the country, who have spent many years in working the same claim, and have spared neither labour nor money in developing their property.

Before leaving Victoria, we had written to Mr. Scott Simpson, the officer in charge at Sylvester's Landing, asking him to have a boat and crew ready for us on our arrival, to take a winter's supply of provisions and other necessaries to Frances Lake, but he had been unable to get a crew for the trip, although he had done his best to persuade any of the good boatmen who were within reach of the trading post to make the expedition. It has become so hard to procure good men for boating that the Company have brought a crew of half-breeds from Winnipeg to boat the trading goods from Dease Lake, rather than rely upon the local Indians, who, besides being untrustworthy, have the strongest aversion to hard work, and expect wages for what little they do at the rates that were in vogue when the diggings were paying and labour was scarce.

Our original intention was to reach Frances Lake as soon as possible, to put up a cabin for winter quarters, and pass the time till spring in hunting moose and exploring the surrounding country. On the last snow we expected to haul the canoe with dog-sleighs across the height of land, and to reach the Pelly, or some of its tributaries, before the break up of the ice. But now our plans were all knocked on the head, as it was evident that our little canoe would not carry enough provisions to enable us to winter in case game should prove scarce, and reach the Pelly in the spring, to say nothing of the ammunition and other weighty necessaries.

We spent a week at the Landing in the hope that some more enterprising Indians might turn up; and then started down stream with no very definite aim in view. Before we left, Simpson promised to send us down a couple of Indians with their sleigh dogs to the Lower Post, at the junction of the Dease with the Liard, at the first opportunity, so that we might haul supplies towards Frances Lake during the winter if we should make up our minds to do so.

CHAPTER IV

THE LIARD POST

Mount Ke-la-gurn—Hyland River—Indian superstitions—Big game in particular localities—First fall of snow.

THE river below MacDame's Creek is very crooked, and during its northerly course of 100 miles or so to its junction with the Liard, has less current than in its upper reaches. As we dropped down stream the mountains receded from the river, and grass benches, lightly clothed with black pine, made their appearance, rising in distinctly marked terraces sometimes to a height of several hundred feet above the river level. In other places the banks were covered with groves of well-grown spruce and cottonwood; and willow was everywhere abundant. Near the mouth of the river are two rapids, each with a clear open channel, but a heavy sea which cannot be avoided; and if the canoe is at all heavily loaded, it is advisable to portage part of the cargo especially in the second rapid. A short way above the first rapid we met a boat-load of prospectors who were coming out after an unsuccessful summer's cruise. Among them was Henry Thibert, who gave us an interesting account of his three years' expedition with M'Culloch from Minnesota to Dease Lake, in the course of which they made the first discovery of gold on the Arctic Slope. After we had done yarning, we inquired about the rapid below, and were told it was good, and that we should have no difficulty in running it on the right side. So without landing to pick out a course, I ran my canoe into the right hand channel, and found that we had entered a shallow rapid with a strong current, absolutely choked with boulders, and no room for the canoe to pass. We bumped two or three times at the upper end, but luckily the crash did not come till we had nearly reached the foot of the bad water. Then a sharp stone tore a hole in the thin planking, the water rose over the bottom boards immediately, and only a hasty landing and discharge of cargo prevented a serious catastrophe. After we had effected repairs, I took a look at the rapid, and found a straight, deep channel on the left side, through which we could have run with perfect ease, if we had not taken the precaution to ask the way beforehand. We took the next rapid cautiously enough, and early on the morning of 1st September reached the Lower Post, a most unpretentious establishment situated on the far side of the Liard, half a mile above the mouth of the Dease. A small store, a log hut for the man in charge, and a few rough buildings belonging to the Indians, make up the last outpost of civilisation in this direction. In charge of the post was a man named Smith, a native of the half-breed settlement of Selkirk in Manitoba, and a capital specimen of his class. His term of contract with the Hudson's Bay Company had nearly run out, and he offered to engage with me for the next summer's expedition to the Yukon if I had to delay my start till the spring. He afterwards proved a most useful bowsman, besides being quiet and thoroughly reliable on emergency. At present he had to look after the trading post till a man was sent to relieve him.

Standing on the bank of a river whose source is unknown, and with a stretch of country lying to the northward several hundred miles in length and breadth, on which the white man has never set his foot, the Liard Post may be regarded as one of the best starting points for exploration of the North-West that are still open to the enthusiastic traveller.

"La Rivière aux Liards" (Cottonwood River) of the early voyageurs, anglicised into the Liard, and further corrupted by the miners into the Deloire, although probably known even by name to comparatively few people, is one of the most important features in the western water system of Canada. Rising, like the Peace, far to the westward of the Rocky Mountains, it cuts through the main range, and, after a wild course of some 800 miles, falls into the Mackenzie at Fort Simpson, mingling its waters with those of the Peace, the Athabasca, and innumerable smaller streams that drain the huge Mackenzie basin.

The Liard can scarcely be called a navigable river, although it has long stretches of quiet water. There are several bad cañons in the upper part of the stream, while the lower river is still worse, and has always enjoyed the reputation of being the most dangerous piece of water in the whole of the Hudson's Bay territory. It was by this route from the Mackenzie that the posts at Fort Halkett, Dease Lake, Frances Lake, and Pelly Banks were supplied fifty years ago; but there were so many disasters from boat accidents and starvation, besides the great cost of keeping up the posts, that the route was abandoned; so that of late years there has been but little intercourse between the two sides of the mountains.

Mr. M'Connell, during the exploratory survey of the extreme North-West made in 1887, ran down stream from the Lower Post to Fort Simpson. He gives a most interesting account of the river and general appearance of the country in his report to the Geological Survey Department.

The Liard Post was our last chance of obtaining Indians, but here we were again disappointed, and decided to postpone our expedition to Frances Lake till the following spring. As there was still a month or six weeks of good canoeing before the cold weather set in, we left the post after a stay of a few hours, with the intention of making a short voyage up Hyland River, a tributary entering the Liard from the north, about 12 miles down stream; and, dropping down with a strong current, we camped for the night just outside the mouth of the smaller river.

The scenery along the Liard is a repetition of that on the Dease, on a larger sale—the same gravel bars and islands, backed by the same pine-covered benches on the banks of the river.

Hyland River was named after Robert Hyland, the first miner who ascended it, in spite of the fact that it had been named the Macpherson many years before by the Hudson's Bay Company's explorers. It appears on some maps as "Highland" River; but if the commonly-used name is to be maintained, it should certainly be allowed its orthography.

Hyland and his party prospected this river some years ago, but the results were not satisfactory. Gold was found on many of the bars, but never in sufficient quantities to pay for working in a country where provisions are so high-priced that four or five dollars to the man is not considered a "grub stake."

For the first few miles the river is swift and broken up into small channels, making the ascent very difficult, but afterwards the current slackens, and there is no obstacle to navigation till the first rapids are reached, at a distance of some 30 miles from the mouth. The direction of the river valley is N.W. to N.N.W., but the stream itself is extremely tortuous. At the rapids the river makes a sharp bend to the eastward, and there are a couple of reaches each a mile in length of really bad water; several ledges of bed rock stretch across the stream, causing steep overfalls; and at one corner the whole force of the current gets on to a high bluff which shoots it off in heavy confused swirls, dangerous to enter even with a big boat. We took the canoe up on the north shore, where there is an inside channel among the rocks which can be worked by a boat of light draught; but even there the current is powerful. At one bluff the line had to be passed down on a float and hauled in from a little bay out of sight from the canoe—always rather a dangerous proceeding, as the roar of the water prevents an order from being heard, and a capsize often happens by keeping too much strain on the line in case of a broad sheer at the edge of an eddy. During the height of the summer floods this must be a hard place to get through. As it was, with the water low in the early part of September, we had to make several portages before reaching the quiet stretch at the head of the rapids.

And now the river became an ideal stream for canoeing—a slack current, with always good tracking on one side, fine weather, and pleasant camping

AN IDEAL STREAM FOR CANOEING.

places, with plenty of dry firewood. The deciduous trees had changed their colour; and the mountains, which began to show up to the northward, were covered with the blue haze which always accompanies the falling of the leaf in these latitudes. Indications of game were not wanting either— moose and bear tracks along the sand bars; beaver chopping among the willows and cottonwood. Geese, ducks, and cranes were in some numbers, too, and the forest was well supplied with spruce grouse and rabbits.

At a distance of 90 miles, by our reckoning, from the mouth, following the bends of the river, the banks contract till they form a cañon several miles in length, with many rapids full of boulders, presenting a formidable impediment to navigation. At the foot of the cañon, a large creek—the only one of any importance that we noticed—joins the Hyland from the eastward, entering between steep cliffs of the same peculiar slate streaked with veins of white and brown quartz that composes the walls of the cañon on the main stream. This tributary is known to the Indians as the Tabathotooa or Bluewater. It rises in a clump of high mountains towards the north-east, and throughout most of its course is a quiet stream winding from side to side of a valley two miles in width. Long afterwards I had occasion to travel along this stream on a winter's journey to the main range of the northern Rockies. In the cañon we put ashore to reconnoitre, with the result that we discovered a high, bare-topped mountain standing at some distance back from the river on the west side, and decided on making an attempt to reach the summit to get a general idea of the country, and to trace the course of the stream as far as we could follow it with the eye from an elevation of several thousand feet. Taking provisions to last us a week, and caching the rest on a scaffold, we pushed on two or three miles with the canoe, portaging, wading, and hauling with lines over the numerous rapids, till we reached the bend of the stream which approached most nearly to the foot of the mountain. Here we landed, and shouldering our blankets and provisions, started through the forest for the bald peak, of which we could occasionally catch a glimpse. The walking was good enough, as there was not much underbush, but the distance was greater than it seemed to be from the river, and it was nearly sundown on the second day when, after some laborious climbing, we reached the summit, and were rewarded with a view that well repaid us for our trouble—a view of wondrous beauty, intensified, perhaps, by the tinge of mystery which always enshrouds the unknown land. Before us, to the north and east, was a vast stretch of country absolutely unexplored; range after range of gently undulating mountain ridges culminating in the distant snow-capped peaks of what we supposed to be the western spurs of the Rocky Mountains. North-west ran the valley of the Hyland River, inclining a little more to the westward just before it disappeared behind a projecting mountain spur. A few miners have ascended the river some distance beyond the point at which we left the cañon, and report it easily navigable above the cañon to its source in a large lake. But the Indians deny the existence of a lake at the head of the river, and say it rises very near to the Frances, as also do the Black River and the Beaver—the two lower tributaries of the Liard, so that the four streams, although wide apart at their mouths, head close together on one plateau, like the ribs of an umbrella. But the Indians do not like the country. Something evil lives there; and once, a long time ago, before the whites came to the Liard, a party of hunters met with a terrible fate at the head-waters of Hyland River. According to the story, they were working their canoe through a cañon when a sudden darkness overtook them, and the evil thing rose out of the water, turned over the canoe, and dragged the unlucky hunters down into the depths of a whirlpool. Since then, the Indians are chary of going far up any of these streams, and turn back, by their own account, as soon as they see bones of huge animals lying on the river bars.

From the top of our mountain, which the Indians call Ke-la-gurn, "the mountain of many sticks," we were now overlooking the approach to this land of evil repute; but the month of September was drawing to its close, and prudence, coupled with the uncertainty as to our winter plans, bade us overcome the desire to push on up the river till a more favourable occasion. Our view to the west and south-west was blocked by high ridges similar to the one on which we stood, but to the southward the Cassiar Range still showed up above the long stretches of undulating forest-covered plateau. Several lakes were in sight, but none of them were of any considerable size, the largest being a sheet of water lying close to the foot of the mountain on the north side, perhaps three miles in length, and drained by a short stream into the Hyland.

There was no large game to be found on the mountain; although in appearance it was a perfect place for cariboo or sheep—long grassy stretches, with straggling clumps of timber, with sometimes a patch of broken rocks or a small precipice; but we saw no sign or track to indicate that animals frequented the mountain at any season of the year. It is a remarkable fact that in these out-of-the-way countries, where one would expect to find game in every favourable spot, the wild animals are extremely local in their distribution. Cariboo certainly travel great distances, but they have their summer and winter ranges, and leave certain districts untraversed, although apparently offering equal inducement in the way of food with the country through which they take their course in their migrations. In the present instance, we learnt afterwards from the Indians that the cariboo are like mosquitoes—the universal Indian synonym for a large number—to the eastward of Hyland River, but do not cross to the west side, while on the Frances the west side is the favoured locality, yet neither of these streams present any obstacle to the cariboo's progress. The mountain sheep are much less inclined to travel if undisturbed, merely changing their elevation according to the season. It is for these reasons that a stranger without local knowledge stands such an uncertain chance of finding game; and may easily waste a month or two in climbing mountains totally unfrequented by animals, when an Indian, familiar with the country from childhood, will make a straight line for the well-known haunts of the game he wishes to hunt.

But birds were plentiful enough on our mountain —spruce grouse, the "fool hen" of the miners, on the lower slopes, blue grouse—the best and largest of all the Canadian grouse family—about the edge of the timber line, and great flocks of ptarmigan in mottled autumn plumage on the sunny side of the open ridges; so that we had no difficulty in keeping the kettle full.

Two nights we passed under the shelter of a clump of spruce timber near the summit; then, having no object in making a longer stay, turned our faces down hill and reached the canoe, in pouring rain, on the fifth day after leaving the river.

The water had risen a foot on account of the heavy rain, and in consequence we had less trouble than we expected in running down the rapids, as we could float over many of the rocks which had been showing above water on our up-stream journey. While pottering about on the shore of the upper cañon to pick out a course for the canoe, I stumbled across a ledge of remarkably pretty blue and white quartz, evidently containing mineral, and broke off a few specimens, which were the cause of my making a winter expedition to the spot to stake off the claim in accordance with the mining statutes.

The run down the Hyland was pleasant and uneventful; we had plenty of provisions and no occasion to hunt with any keenness. We met nobody, although we saw several spruce bark canoes hauled up on the banks in different places. The Cascas and Liard Indians are poor boatmen, and do not make much use of the waterways, preferring to pack heavy loads through the woods to working a canoe up stream; while, if they wish to run down a river, they can make a bark or skin canoe in a few hours, and lose nothing by throwing it away at the end of the run. The birch on the Upper Liard does not grow to a sufficient size to supply bark suitable for the canoes so much used on the lower part of the river.

The first fall of snow occurred on 20th September, and a couple of days afterwards we arrived at the Lower Post. Here we met a Californian mining expert, who had come into the country on purpose to examine a quartz ledge on Hyland River. Some samples of wonderfully rich ore, said to have come from this ledge, had reached his office in San Francisco; and although it was already late in the year to start on such a long journey, he had set out at once to see if there was any truth in the story. He returned to the Lower Post after spending a couple of weeks on Hyland River, just in time to get out before the ice began to run; and was so mysteriously reticent as to what he had seen that quartz ledges were the talk of the winter from the banks of the Liard to Fort Wrangel. Gladman, our Canadian bowsman, went out with him, being anxious to reach civilisation before winter set in. He had told me before leaving that he would be unable to go the whole journey, as he had an engagement in Ottawa for the early spring. I was sorry to lose his services for the next summer, as he was a good man in the bow and a very handy boat-builder and carpenter. As no Indians had yet turned up, Reed and I pitched our lodge about 10 miles up stream, at the head of a long cañon, which is no doubt a wild stretch of river during the summer floods, but at low water is fairly easy to navigate. Here we awaited results, and occupied our time in getting out logs and putting up a cabin which would serve us for winter quarters if necessary, besides making occasional moose hunts; but we soon found out from the absence of tracks that we had chosen a hopeless piece of country to hunt in. There were plenty of grouse and rabbits to keep us in food, and two or three weeks slipped away pleasantly enough. Then a cold snap started the ice running in the river, snow lay several inches deep on the ground, and it seemed that winter had come already, but it was a false alarm; in a few days the snow had gone and the river was clear of ice for another three weeks.

CHAPTER V

MOOSE HUNTING

The country south of Liard River—Civilised Indians—Increase of number of moose—Habits of the moose.

ON 18th October we went into the post and found the Hudson's Bay boat had arrived from Sylvester's Landing, with Simpson himself on board, also two Indians with their wives and families, who professed themselves to be willing to stay with us for the winter and do any work we required of them in the way of moose hunting, or hauling supplies up the Liard towards Frances Lake.

We learned that several important changes had taken place in the little world of Cassiar through the action of the Hudson's Bay officials in Victoria. The great corporation had come to the conclusion that its business in Cassiar was not remunerative, and had decided to sell out all interests to a free-trader named La Montagne, who had been for some years opposing the Company in the fur trade with an establishment on the Liard, 90 miles below the Lower Post. The Manitoba half-breeds, who had been employed in boating on the Dease, were to be discharged after the winter, and two of them had volunteered to go with me in the spring to the Yukon, and take their chance of eventually reaching the sea coast in preference to being sent direct to Wrangel on the breaking up of the ice.

This was most satisfactory news to me, as Reed had made up his mind to remain in Cassiar another summer, and I had become very doubtful whether I should be able to get any men for the trip. Now I could rely on the half-breeds, and be quite independent of the Indians should they all refuse their services, as usually happens when they are called upon to make a journey beyond the limits of their own country.

The boat left immediately for La Montagne's trading post, and a few days afterwards we started for a moose hunt on the level bench country to the west of the Dease and south of the Liard. It was rather a bad season to set out, as there was no snow to enable us to travel with dog-sleighs and snow-shoes, yet at any time snow might fall heavily and make travelling by any other method a matter of great difficulty. As we had no snow-shoes ready, we determined to take our chance, and sallied forth with loads on our backs and a couple of dogs, heavily packed, in attendance.

Very peculiar individuals were our two Indians, Charley and Two-fingered Johnny—so named from a malformation of one hand; a couple of good examples of what might have been rather fine characters if they had never come into contact with the bastard civilisation of the mining camp. I don't believe the red man was ever the noble creature he has often been painted. We can only suppose that in time past he led a harmless existence, and unconsciously did his duty in the particular station of life to which he had been called; but, dress him up in the white man's clothes, feed him on bacon and flour, canned peaches, and molasses, give him a few drinks of whisky, and he becomes a despicable brute. He does not like being taken away from all these good things, and has a profound contempt for the few true Indians who still make a living in the woods by trapping the precious fur. So it was with Charlie and Johnny. They were good enough men to track a moose, or work round the camp; but on all the trips we went with them their hearts were never in the life—they did everything sulkily, quarrelled with each other, and grumbled because

A WINTER CAMP.

there was no canned fruit; while their women would on no account go to the woods to dry meat or cure skins—they were not that sort of women, they told us, but must dress in the finest that could be bought in the store and sit through the glorious winter weather by the side of a sheet-iron stove.

We wandered casually through the forest, camping wherever night overtook us, hunting for a day or two from each camp, and then moving on to fresh ground. If we killed, the meat was cut up and stowed away in strong log caches built on the spot, to be hauled into the fort whenever it was wanted. Moose were plentiful; we killed eleven during the three weeks that we were out—this, too, without any very energetic hunting. Besides rabbits, and the attendant lynx, there were a good many porcupines, fat and easily killed by following a fresh track. These were objects of greater interest to our Indians than the moose, which are by no means a certainty, and often lead to much hard walking without any result. The porcupines really are most excellent eating at this time of year; but in the spring and summer, when they have lost their fat, their flesh is only tolerable under the pressure of necessity.

Snow fell frequently while we were out, and by the end of the first week in November it was deep enough for snow-shoeing, so we were forced to give up our hunt till we were better equipped for winter work. To reach the fort, we cut across to the Liard, intending to build a raft and run the

20 miles down stream; but when we came out on the south bank the river was full of running ice, and we saw at once that we should have to continue our journey on foot. It was a long and difficult walk, through fallen timber, while the snowfall was already 18 inches in depth. Added to this there was a chance of not being able to cross the river at the Lower Post, but when we reached this point we were glad to find that the ice had jammed in the cañon, leaving the water comparatively open below, so that we could cross in a boat without trouble.

Twenty-five years ago there were very few moose along the Liard, and the animal was unknown to the Indians hunting to the westward of Dease Lake. Then there began to be frequent rumours of a big track seen in the snow, and momentary glimpses of a beast whose size varied according to the fancy of the startled hunter. Then a young brave stood face to face with a moose, and slew it; and the Cascas discovered that a new animal —larger and better than anything they knew before —had invaded their country. To-day, the little-known region drained by the Dease, the Upper Liard, the Frances, and the Pelly, is probably the best moose country on the continent of North America. Where did all these moose come from? and how far will they extend their wanderings towards the west? Quite recently there were none between Dease Lake and Telegraph Creek Lake; now moose are killed every year close to Telegraph Creek; and there are even reports of tracks having been seen as far down as the Little Cañon of the Stikine. Northward, too, they extend, in increasing numbers, down the Great Yukon as far as the junction of the Tanana, and up the latter stream to its head.

There is a theory that the moose have been driven away from Peace River and the Lower Liard, and have crossed the mountains to Cassiar to avoid the continual hunting to which they are subjected on the east side. But, as a matter of fact, there is very little hunting done in that part of the country, as the Indians are not numerous, and are rapidly dying out, besides depending more and more every year on the provisions imported to the Peace River trading posts. Whatever may be the reason of this migration, it gives me the greatest pleasure to be able to report that, at this late date, when from almost every part of the world the cry arises that the wild animals are being exterminated, there is still a remote corner where the noblest animal of the whole deer family is increasing and multiplying at an almost incredible rate.

And this state of affairs is likely to continue. The miner, having scraped out all the gold dust he could find in the creeks and on the river bars, has gone to seek new fields, leaving behind him the dread diseases which must infallibly kill out the native population. Then the moose will have everything their own way; the cariboo and sheep will roam unmolested on the mountain tops; and the country will relapse into the vast game preserve for which it is so eminently suited. As soon as the snow goes off in the spring, the moose comes out into the low-lying swamps and along the river banks, in search of the young shoots of the willow which constitute its principal food throughout the year. In the heat of the summer it frequents the open gravel bars, and may often be seen swimming across the rivers, or standing up to its belly in the cool waters of a lake. The rutting season begins about the middle of September, when the bulls travel continually and at a rapid pace in search of the cows, which are then ranging in the elevated country back from the rivers—often far up the mountain sides, in the willow-covered swamps where the little creeks have their sources. Here the moose remain till the deep snow drives them down to the lower ground, and eventually back to the river banks, where, if undisturbed, they pass the cold months without wandering far from some backwater or slough running up into the woods they have selected for winter quarters.

The old bulls shed their horns in the beginning of January, the young ones a month later. The horns of a young bull killed on the 1st of February dropped off in my hands when I was dragging the carcass clear of the bushes to skin it. On 9th May the new growth of horns in a full-grown bull protruded about an inch from the head. The young are dropped in the beginning of June; the cows and calves being usually found among the thick growth of willows along the river banks at that season.

Where moose are plentiful, they are not difficult to kill; and none of the Dease and Liard Indians would be considered expert hunters on the east side of the Rockies, where these animals are scarce and really hard to approach; and if a moose is driven

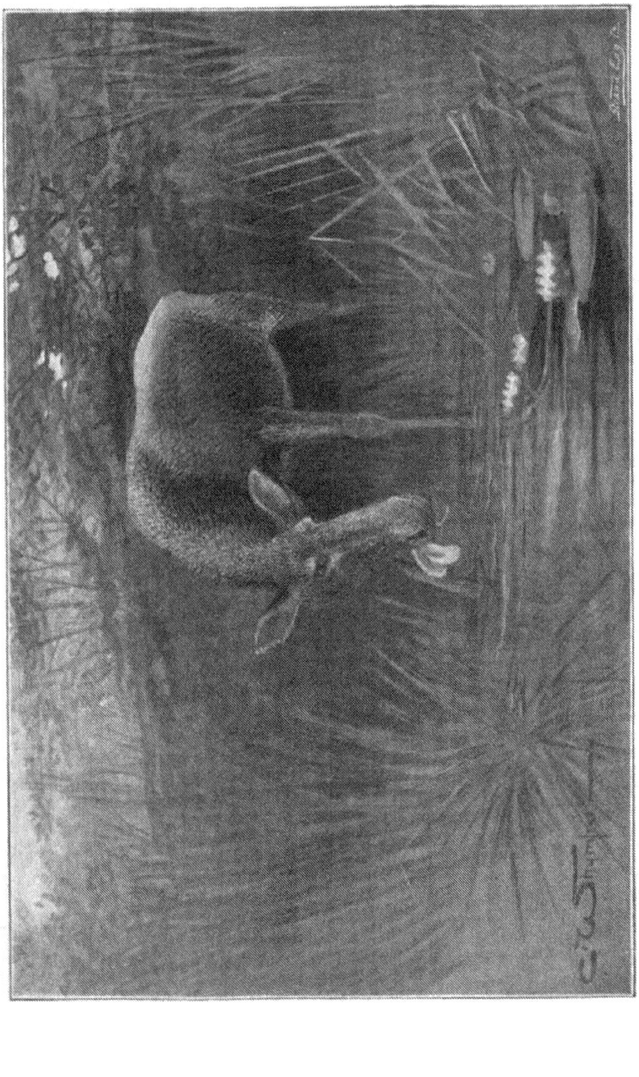

away through carelessness, it may be some time before another chance is offered. But the Cassiar Indians know that they can always find another fresh track if they disturb the first moose, and consequently do not always use due precaution in approaching their game. Another reason for their inferiority as hunters is, that they are never really dependent on their guns for a living; and if they have a dollar or two—or, better still, a little credit—they prefer buying canned beef from the nearest store to hunting meat in the woods.

In March and April, when the snow is deep, the moose are easily run down by a man on big snowshoes, and can often be driven in any direction the hunter pleases. The usual method is to drive the animal on to the river ice before killing him, to avoid the trouble of taking the sleighs into the timber to bring out the meat. The snow is seldom deep enough in this country to force the moose to yard, as is their habit in Nova Scotia and New Brunswick; so the system of wholesale slaughter which was formerly practised in the Eastern Provinces is impossible in Cassiar; nor do the Indians here seem to have any knowledge of calling the moose during the rutting season—a method much in vogue among the Mic-Macs; but they occasionally attract the attention of an old bull by scraping a bone against the bark of a tree, and thus imitating the sound of a rival polishing his horns.

CHAPTER VI

HAULING STORES TO FRANCES LAKE

Ice set fast in the rivers—Cassiar sleigh dogs—Disease among the Liard Indians—Ideal day for a hunt—Difficulties of hauling supplies—Dangers of a really cold day—A process of freezing out.

By the middle of November the ice had set fast in the rivers, and snow-shoes and dog-sleighs were in fashion. Cassiar dogs are by no means true representatives of the northern race of hauling dogs, but show unmistakable signs of having civilised blood in their veins. Instead of the native semi-wolf of the Esquimaux and the Indians of the Mackenzie River, all the well-known civilised breeds may be recognised in various stages of degradation. Mongrel mastiffs, retrievers, setters, and pointers are the most frequent types to be met with, showing that the race is the offspring of any large dogs that could be stolen from the streets of San Francisco or Victoria just before the steamers started with their loads of miners bound for the Cassiar goldfields. We made several short moose hunts—some successful and some otherwise—coming into the post for a few days and then going off into the woods for a fortnight. We went in every direction—down the Liard, up the Liard, and up the Dease, but everywhere we found the same abundance of moose tracks. Once we visited a large lake 20 miles to the westward of the post, and laid in a supply of whitefish, which we caught in nets under the ice, in great quantities. Here we found a band of Liard Indians hunting and fishing. Sickness was prevalent in the camp—very few of the men were well enough to hunt moose, and they had come to the lake to be sure of making a living. A melancholy spectacle the camp presented; half a dozen pits in the snow lined with pine brush, a little more pine brush stuck up as a wind-break, and no other shelter from the weather. Lying in their blankets were the sick men, some of them evidently never to get up again—dying among the moose hair and fish guts that were liberally scattered over everything; and outside the filth of the camp the ice-bound lake sparkled in the winter sunshine that always seems so full of health and strength.

What was the matter with them all? "Oh! we're always like this," the chief explained, "since the white men came to the country. In the old time, my tribe was powerful, but now many of my people die every winter. Some children are born, but they are no good—they die soon."

Now, in the interests of ethnology, if not of humanity, would it not be worth somebody's while to send a qualified doctor to patch up as best he might the remnants of the tribes of the Casca and Liard Indians, and prevent the spread of contagion? A good deal of money is spent annually by the Dominion and the various Provincial Governments in doing whatever is done for the Indians of Canada —surely a little might be spared for this outlying part of the country; and let the man whose salary it pays be a doctor and not an Indian agent. No surveys are wanted; no reservations need be staked off; for, if the present state of affairs continues but a few more years, extinction will put every Indian beyond the limitation of the agent's reserve.

The winters in Cassiar are mild in comparison to the climate in the same latitude to the eastward of the Rockies. The warm Chinook winds from the Pacific penetrate the Coast Ranges, modifying the intensity of the cold to such an extent that there is usually a thaw with rainfall during some part of the winter. Snow falls frequently but not heavily, and there is less sunshine than in the eastern winters, but there are occasional cold snaps when the thermometer falls extremely low, the weather being then always bright and calm.

Frequent hunting trips made the weeks go by quickly till the shortest day was passed. This is always considered the turning point of the winter in the North, although in reality most of the cold weather comes after the new year.

There is an indescribable charm in this winter hunting in the great northern woods—waste of time and unnecessary hardship, as many people would call it. I never know quite what the attraction is; but after a couple of days' comfort and high living in a house, some feeling of restlessness is sure to drive you out into the snow and its attendant discomforts if you have any trace of the original savage left in your nature. The mere fact of being in the woods is sufficient to appease this craving. The actual killing of the moose is a minor point —unless you are short of provisions, and then the shot is taken anxiously enough.

One of the pleasantest hunts I remember was taken from a camp 20 miles up the Dease, where I spent a week with Beavertail Johnny—a much better fellow than his two-fingered namesake—hunting moose and setting traps for lynx.

BURNT TIMBER IN WINTER.

New Year's Eve was an ideal day for our sport. A gale of wind was blowing and light snow falling—the time when the big ears of the moose are blocked with snow, and he hears nothing but the loudest cracking of the branches; while on a clear cold day the least sound is audible, and the creaking of the babiche lacing of the snow-shoes is loud enough to alarm the moose at a long distance. We had plodded along on snow-shoes up and down the rolling hills to the southward of the river, but it was well on towards evening when we discovered fresh tracks. Two moose had passed just ahead of us, and it was a question whether we could catch them up before dark. An hour was spent in following the tracks, and at last we saw the animals slowly crossing an open ridge a few hundred yards away. As soon as they disappeared, we started at our best speed, and came upon our game at close range, nipping the willow twigs that grew thickly on the other side of the summit. The shot was not easy in the falling snow and rapidly increasing darkness, but I dropped one, and there was a little blood in the track of the other. And then the wind fell suddenly, the snow stopped, and the full moon shone out brightly, lighting up the snow-laden spruce trees and willow bushes, with the distant peaks of the Cassiar range in the background. We skinned and cut up the moose by moonlight, and started back for the river with a sufficient supply for supper, picking out the best road as we went, for our tracks would be hard enough in the morning to enable us to haul out the rest of the meat with the dog-sleighs. It was late when we reached the camp, and were heartily welcomed by the dogs, who knew in an instant that we had killed a moose, and that there was a good time coming for a few days.

A big kettle of fat meat brought the day to an end, and the New Year found us with our heads under the blankets and our feet stretched out to the blazing fire.

The next day we brought in the meat, and followed the blood-track for several miles; but the moose was evidently not much hurt, as he had never laid down, and presently the blood ceased altogether.

In the middle of January, La Montagne came up to the Lower Post and left for Victoria, giving us a chance of sending out letters, and promising to be back by the beginning of April. Reed went with him to Dease Lake, and at the end of the month I thought it advisable to begin hauling supplies up the Liard towards Frances Lake; so, late one afternoon, I left the post with four dog-sleighs loaded with all the provisions I could lay hands on, accompanied by three of the Manitoba half-breeds sent down from Sylvester's Landing by Simpson, and a good little Indian named Secatz in place of Charlie, who was, or pretended to be, too ill to travel. The weather set in cold from the start, and continued so for a fortnight—the only really cold snap that we had all the winter. The travelling with heavy loads was slow, as we had to go ahead every day to break the road through the snow, and wait till the night's frost hardened up our tracks before the dogs could pull the sleighs. In the soft snow we could make no headway at all, but sometimes we found long stretches of glare ice which helped us greatly. A good deal of time, too, was taken up in hunting, as, unless we killed moose, we had to fall back on our loads of provisions that were intended for use many months afterwards.

It took us a week or more to reach the mouth of the Frances River, which joins the Liard from the north 45 miles above the Lower Post. It enters by two channels, one on either side of a large island; and might easily be missed in the winter time, as the Liard is here much broken up by islands and gravel bars.

Only two moose had been killed, and the weather

still increased in severity. 2nd February was the coldest day of the whole winter, the thermometer at Dease Lake, 200 miles to the southward, as we afterwards heard, standing at −68° Fahr. Secatz and I left camp before daylight that morning to hunt, leaving orders with the half-breeds to haul the loads up to the island, as we had broken the road ahead overnight. At the mouth of the Frances we separated, Secatz hunting along the Frances while I followed the Liard for several miles. I found two fresh moose tracks, but could not get a shot; and it was long after dark when I reached the island again, fully expecting to find the cargo all up and the camp made. But there was no sign of anybody, except that the rifle which Secatz had been using was stuck up in the snow where the road left the ice and turned up the bank. With the aid of a match I examined the road and saw that no sleighs had passed, and Secatz's snowshoe tracks were leading down stream. It was only then that I realised how fearfully cold it was. I had eaten nothing since early morning, and had been sweating while running after the moose, always a bad thing to do in cold weather, as you are sure to get chilled as soon as you stop for a minute.

I expected to find the camp close, so would not wait to light a fire, but left my rifle and started down stream at a run. I could never get warm again, although I had still ten miles to go; and my nose and cheeks were rather badly frozen before I saw the glare of the camp fire through the trees. I found the half-breeds having a good time, sitting round the fire rolled up in blankets, drinking tea and shouting the chorus of a highly improper song long popular in the Red River Settlements. They had only moved camp about a mile, as they began to freeze, and could not get the dogs along quickly enough to keep themselves warm; so they had put ashore and made a fire as soon as they saw dry wood enough to camp with. Secatz had come in just ahead of me, with the same experience as myself—a frozen nose and no moose meat.

In this extreme cold it is never really safe for a man to go into the woods alone, as, if he meets with an accident severe enough to cripple him, or gets wet by breaking through a weak spot in the ice, he is absolutely certain to freeze to death unless he is very quick in lighting a fire. In any case he should always carry an axe in his belt and plenty of matches, so that he may still have a chance if dry wood is close at hand. One of the greatest dangers lies in the fact that your fingers are likely to freeze, or at least become useless for lighting a match, as soon as you grasp the handle of an axe and impede the free circulation of the blood, as a layer of ice is sure to have formed between the moose-skin and the inside lining of your mittens. This sort of weather is good enough for travelling straight ahead on a good road with light loads on the sleighs, but in this case our dogs were overloaded, and the snow was so soft that we could not keep warm while travelling slowly.

At night we were comfortable enough, as we kept a big fire going. It was at first the coldest man's business to put on wood, but this led to trouble, and I finally had to establish a regular watch. One of the common tricks of a winter camp is the habit men have of pretending to be sleeping, warm and snug, in the hopes of freezing some other poor devil out of his blankets to make up the fire. You can get up shaking with cold, and throw on big sticks from the wood pile, chop kindling, and make as much noise as you like, yet not a soul will be sufficiently awake to lend you a hand. But as soon as the fire burns up brightly, and the kettle begins to boil, the least rattle of a spoon against a tin cup will rouse the whole camp as readily as a gunshot. The cup of tea in the small hours of these shivering mornings, with the return of warmth and the prospect of a few more hours' sleep, is one of the most pleasant recollections of northern travel, bringing back to the memory the intense brilliancy of the stars, the dim outline of the mountains, and the deathly silence of the snow-laden forest and ice-bound river.

At the mouth of the Frances we were completely stranded, as the ice was flooded under the snow, and there was no chance of keeping our feet dry enough to avoid freezing. Camp was made on the island, and here we stayed for four days hunting moose; but in this respect, too, we were out of luck, owing to the great cold. It was impossible to get about in the woods without making enough noise with our snow-shoes to scare away the most confiding of animals. Even the rabbits refused to let us get near them; and, seeing that we should be obliged to broach our cargo if we remained longer, a strong cache was built and everything stowed away safely till a more favourable opportunity turned up. Then, with the advantage of a hard road and light sleighs, we turned our faces down stream, and soon covered the 45 miles to the Lower Post, arriving there in straggling order, according to each individual's staying powers.

CHAPTER VII

A MINING EXPEDITION

Return to Sylvester's Landing for summer supplies—Rabbits and grouse—Murder by Casca Indians—Expedition to Hyland River—Quartz ledges—Chesi Hill, the home of the big-horn—Jealousy between Cassiar Indians and Red River half-breeds.

My next expedition was made in company with Beavertail Johnny and Secatz, to the Hudson's Bay Company's headquarters at Sylvester's Landing, to get additional supplies for the summer. The usual winter road follows the Dease for 30 miles, and then strikes off to the eastward, passing through an open grassy country, with numerous lakes, and skirting the foot of a high range known as the Horse Ranche Mountains. It is here that the horses used for packing provisions to the outlying mining camps in the summer pass the long winter, scraping away the snow in search of the bunch-grass, usually coming out in good condition in the spring, although once or twice things have gone wrong, and many of the band were missing when the snow went off.

On the long portage between the two big lands of the Dease, rabbits were in great numbers. We killed thirty-five one day with our rifles without stopping to hunt away from the road, besides several spruce grouse—and this too with a penalty of a plug of tobacco for everything shot in the body. The rabbits are as white as the snow, and at first are hard to see till they run, but after a little practice the round black eye is spotted at once, and there is usually plenty of time for a shot. The spruce grouse is a most confiding bird, and will rarely leave its bough till its head is cut off by a bullet. Moose are seldom found far back from the river in this part of the country, as there is not much willow for them to feed on. The Horse Ranche Mountains used to be a good place for cariboo, but they were so much hunted when meat could be sold for a big price to the MacDame Creek miners, that they are now only to be found here during the spring and autumn migrations.

We set traps for lynx as we went, and picked up several on the way back. In a good rabbit year lynx are always plentiful, and are the simplest of animals to trap or snare. The Casca Indians have the greatest objection to white men trapping on their own account in their country; gold dust they can take as much as they like, but the fur is the Indian's equivalent for gold, and must be left for the Indian. They are very firm on this point —so much so that a couple of white men who were trapping on the Liard some years ago were killed by the Indians because they refused to let the fur alone. They were repeatedly warned, and their traps knocked down or sprung every time they set them, but they persisted in bringing their fate upon themselves. The details of the murder are, I believe, partially known, and several Indians are still living who were implicated in the killing, but very little was done by the authorities to inquire into the matter.

At the end of the long portage we crossed the Dease again, having cut off its big westerly bend, and immediately dived into the woods on the other side, and, crossing seven or eight lakes that lie in a narrow pass between high mountains, reached the hard-beaten track from the Landing to MacDame's Creek mining camp. Another 8 miles took us to the fort. The total distance by the winter road, from the Lower Post to Sylvester's Landing, is not more than 75 miles—a great saving on the circuitous course of 110 miles pursued by the Dease.

At the fort I found Simpson, who was just then very keen on quartz ledges and mining generally. He had come to the conclusion that the specimens of quartz I had brought down from Hyland River were of great value, and, as there was little fur-trading to be done at Sylvester's Landing just at present, he proposed that we should go and stake off a claim according to the mining regulations, and take possession of a property that would quickly make our fortunes. It was only 150 miles or so from where we were. The snow was beginning to harden, and the days were getting long enough to enable us to make a good day's journey; so I at once agreed, and it was arranged that I should go ahead to the Lower Post, with our heavily loaded sleighs, and Simpson should join me there in a few days, as he had some work to finish before he could leave. Accordingly, the next day I went to "town" as the mining camp is called, to lay in my supplies. The winter road followed the valley of MacDame's Creek closely, and was so hard from frequent trail that we could run on it without snow-shoes. About 10 miles up we came to China Bar, a collection of cabins occupied by the Chinamen who are still mining on the creek. A little farther on is the "town,"— mere log cabins, now deserted, but once the scene of great activity, and for a brief period a really paying camp. Now the sole resident is Mr. Buckley, an old timer, who keeps a store for the few white men who are working some distance above. Here I found I could get everything I wanted in the way of provisions, and also, on payment of five dollars, obtained a mining license, setting forth that I was a free miner of the Cassiar district, and giving me the right of ownership to any claim that I might consider it worth while to stake off in legal manner.

Thus provided, we set out with the sleighs, and reached the Lower Post without event a day or two ahead of Simpson. It was now the beginning of March, and I saw that I must do something towards getting my supplies up to Frances Lake while I was away on the prospecting expedition, or we might be overtaken by an early spring and delayed by the breaking up of the ice. Accordingly, one of the half-breeds was despatched up the Liard with Beavertail Johnny and Secatz, taking all the available dogs to move the loads by slow stages up to the lake, and wherever possible to provide against future emergency by killing moose. I was to start, hauling the canoe, as soon as I returned from Hyland River, and expected to overtake the advance party at Frances Lake.

The days were long and the sun was getting powerful when Simpson and I left the post, accompanied by a half-breed and the Indian, Charley. We struck out in a northerly direction, with the intention of falling on the Hyland River some 30 miles from its mouth, instead of making the long detour by following the course of the stream. A series of steep broken hills, covered with burnt timber and the new growth of pine, made hard travelling at first, but about 5 miles out we reached a chain of small lakes separated by short portages, and, of course, were able to make much better headway. Early on the second day we came to the bank of the river a couple of bends below the first cañon. Here we found the snow deep, and the travelling became slow again. We usually camped at midday, and each man took his turn to walk ahead as far as possible to make the road for the following day. With further delays to hunt meat whenever necessity arose, eight days were occupied in reaching the upper cañon, where the ledge was situated; and then we could not carry out our prospecting with any great accuracy, as the snow covered the ground to the depth of 4 feet. The cañon looked very grand in its winter garb, but there was an ugly roar of swirling water under our feet as we carefully picked our way round the steep bluffs, and the ice was dangerous in places. A difficulty arose, too, in the scarcity of provisions, and we were down to starvation point when Charlie killed a moose, and saved us from beating a hasty retreat upon a supply of meat we had left 50 miles down stream for our return journey. Finally we succeeded in marking off our claim, driving our stakes on what appeared to our limited knowledge to be most likely ground, and secured enough rock specimens to make an assay from. I have since learnt that these specimens proved to be fairly rich in silver and to contain a little gold, but not enough to justify the heavy expense of transporting mining machinery to such a distance from salt water. Several claims have been taken up in the neighbourhood during the past summer; but there seems little chance of these far-off ledges ever being worked to advantage, unless some of them should prove to be fabulously rich as they are opened up.

Having accomplished our purpose, we lost no time in making our way back to the post, which we reached early on the fourth day, as little snow had fallen and the road was in good condition. The sun was strong in the middle of the day, and the snow began to ball on our snow-shoes; so we travelled early and late to take advantage of the frost, and made long halts at noon.

At the Lower Post we found Reed, who had been hunting cariboo between Dease Lake and the Stikine, and had fully made up his mind to spend the summer in Cassiar. La Montagne was not expected back for a fortnight; and, as he was to bring my letters from Victoria, I decided to take the canoe and the rest of my summer supplies to Frances Lake and then make a hurried trip back to the post to meet him, thus making sure that everything should be at the lake before the ice broke up on the Liard and Frances, although this arrangement would give me an extra journey of 300 miles. The ice in the lake would continue sound long after the river had broken up, while there would probably be sufficient snow in the woods to enable us to use sleighs in crossing the height of land between Frances Lake and the head of the Pelly.

On the 27th March I left the post with the Indian, Charley, and one of the Manitoba half-breeds, Alick Flett, who had been with us on the Hyland. The canoe proved rather an awkward load for a dog-sleigh, especially on rough ice. Where the travelling was good she rode fairly well; but whenever the sleigh ran a little off the track, the outside runner buried itself in the soft snow, and a capsize was usually the result. On the third day we reached the mouth of the Frances, and found that all the cargo had been moved forward, and the cache was filled with the meat of two moose which our hunters had killed close to the bank of the river. This enabled us to push on without the delay necessary for hunting our own provisions; and, as our advance party had been in luck with the moose, we found meat in several of their camps along the road.

The Frances River is extremely crooked near its junction with the Liard, but Secatz had made portages wherever anything could be gained by so doing. Unfortunately, with the Indian's prudence, he had cut the road only wide enough to let his own sleigh pass; and the extra width of the canoe entailed a good deal of chopping among the pine trees. The banks, too, were almost precipitous, and great care was necessary to prevent the canoe taking charge in some of the steep hills at the end of the portages.

Our general direction was N.N.W., and the appearance of the river banks, and in fact the whole surrounding country, was so exactly like the scenery of Hyland River that the half-breed Alick recognised several places seen on the latter stream, and came to the conclusion that we had entered the Hyland by some other mouth. The positions of the cañons, too, closely correspond, and even the False Cañon on the Frances is faintly indicated by a small rapid on the Hyland. At the upper cañon, on each stream, the rivers make the same sharp bend to the eastward in their descent, and offer the suggestion that the geological obstructions to their easy courses are continued through the country between the two streams.

Just above the first cañon on the Frances, the wide forest-covered plateaux begin to give way to the mountain ranges, and here low rounded hills with little timber show up on the east bank. One of these hills, known to the natives as "Chesi," was once a sure find for big-horn, but a few years ago, during a season of deep snow, they were nearly all killed by a band of Pelly River Indians, who made themselves very unpopular with the Liard tribes in consequence of this breach of the hunting laws, which require each hunter to keep within his own territory. Any sheep that survived the raid have since avoided Chesi and sought security in the higher ranges to the north.

We found an encampment of Indians 40 miles up from the mouth of the river, and obtained from them a supply of moccasins and babiche that we were rather short of. They also gave us a general description of the country, and the localities of the game. Some of the hunters had just returned from an expedition to the Simpson Mountains, lying at some distance to the westward of the Frances. They pointed us out some round-topped mountains where the cariboo were particularly numerous. The best moose country, they told us, lies to the eastward of the False Cañon—a constriction of the river without rapids, a few miles above their camp. From the False Cañon it is an Indian's "not far" to Hyland River, a large lake occupying most of the space between the two streams. Simpson Lake—so named by Campbell many years ago—is drained by the upper of two creeks coming in from the westward below the False Cañon, but does not nearly approach Frances Lake in size. Our informants also told us that we should be wise to leave the canoe above the upper cañon, as the head of the river is open in the spring long before the ice has begun to move on the Liard and Lower Frances. If we had to return to the trading post, we might afterwards find the canoe most necessary for reaching the lake. We acted on this advice, as the ice seemed already a little unsound in the upper cañon, and with lighter loads on the sleighs we caught up our advance party within a few miles of the lake, on the eighth day's travel from the post.

Secatz told us they had been having a good enough time of it, killing moose without much trouble, and making double trips with the cargoes. He had been making the road ahead that day, but had not seen the lake, although from what the Indians had told us it could not be far away. On the following morning we loaded everything on the five sleighs and went to the end of the road, within a couple of miles of the lake, as we afterwards found out. Here we built a large cache, and, having stowed the whole cargo as securely as possible, started to retrace our steps to the Lower Post. By steady walking on a good track, we covered the distance of 145 miles in four days, the halts being enlivened by rather formidable quarrels between the Indians and the half-breeds. On the last night out I had great difficulty in keeping the peace, and possibly guns and axes would have been called into play if we had had much farther to go.

The importation of the Red River half-breeds has caused a good deal of jealousy among the Cassiar Indians, and they seldom make a journey together without more or less rows, arising usually from very trivial causes. The present generation of Indians have seen plenty of rough fighting and brutality among the worst class of miners, and the half-breeds have never known anything much better, so that a quarrel which starts with the kicking of heads and biting of noses may easily lead to a most disastrous finish.

CHAPTER VIII

START FOR THE PELLY RIVER

La Montagne's arrival on 18th April. The Liard chief's theory of the Unknown—Journey up Frances River—Frances Lake—The legend of the flying cariboo—Pelly Indians—Yus-ez-uh River—More stories of cannibals across the divide.

LA MONTAGNE had not yet returned from the coast, and as Smith—who was coming with me—had still charge of the post, I felt bound to wait as long as I possibly could. Of course every day would weaken the ice and lessen our chance of getting to the Pelly on the snow. We had not long to wait, however. La Montagne turned up within a few days of our arrival, and having answered letters and settled all business, we made a final start for the north on 18th April. My crew now consisted of Smith, Archie and Alick Flett, cousins, and Secatz, who was to come with us as interpreter till we reached the Pelly. The other Indians had all refused to go, but Secatz was willing to take the risk of coming back alone in case he should not fall in with any of his friends on their way in to the post to trade their winter's catch of fur. Charlie and Beavertail Johnny at the last minute offered to come with us, but I had now no use for their services, so they were obliged to go to the woods for a living till the summer, when they expected to get employment in the traders' boats. I have heard since that they both died during the following winter. Charlie will be very little loss, as he was acknowledged by whites and Indians alike to be utterly worthless, but Johnny was, next to Secatz, about the best of the Liard Indians.

The two half-breeds were willing enough fellows, not over-burdened with sense, and absolutely useless as hunters, but always cheery and ready to do what they were told, which is really saying a good deal, as men of their class usually have their own ideas how everything should be done, and get sulky if they are not allowed their own way.

By this time there was not much darkness, and the night and early morning, while the frost lasted, were the only times when travel was possible. In the heat of the day the snow was melting rapidly and the dogs could make no headway with the sleighs. We were more heavily loaded than we ought to have been, considering that our summer's supplies were already at Frances Lake; but, as usual, there were many things forgotten till the last moment, and many things that were afterwards thrown away on account of their weight, which might just as well have been left at the post.

In the spring, just before the ice breaks up, is the pleasantest time of all for travelling with dogs. A sharp frost in the night makes a hard crust over which the sleighs run without trouble, and a quick step can be kept up with little exertion. When the sun gets strong in the morning, you can put ashore and sleep through the heat of the day, unless provisions are low, in which case everybody must turn out and hunt moose or small game. On this occasion we had meat scattered all along our road, and beyond killing a few rabbits when we found them especially plentiful, we did no hunting till we reached the lake.

The ice was weak enough by this time. The old road had collapsed in many places, leaving stretches of open water in its stead; and on 20th April we saw the first sign of the wild-fowl returning, a single golden-eye swimming in one of these pools. A few more days brought the mallard, widgeon, and teal, but the geese and swans were much later in arriving. The woods were full of small spring birds, and hawks and owls were in great abundance.

At the mouth of the Frances we met the Liard Chief with his band of Indians, and from them secured a guide, who told us he knew the country to the north of Frances Lake perfectly, and would show us a short route to the Pelly. He described this route so thoroughly that I thought he must really know something about it, till we reached the end of Frances Lake, which we could, of course, have found easily enough for ourselves. Here our guide told us he had come to the end of his country and knew no more.

The Liard Chief was full of anxiety for our welfare, and advised us to turn back at once, or we should surely come to an untimely end at the hands of the savages who inhabit the head-waters of the Pelly. Such is the Indian's nature; anything he does not know and has not seen is bad. No doubt, many years ago the Pellys and the Liards used to fight each other as frequently as did all the other northern tribes, but in these days the chance meetings between the Indians from the different sides of the watershed are extremely friendly. But far up among the mountains, the chief told us, there dwelt a band of cannibals, who would slay any intruder into their country more cheerfully than they would kill a moose. The foundation for this rumour seems to have been the disappearance of a miner named Munro, who pushed out alone on a prospecting trip towards the Pelly, and was no more heard of. The Indians assume that he was killed by a nomadic band of hunters, who have since been afraid to come into any of the widely scattered Hudson's Bay Posts, and do their trading with the other Indians they may encounter in their wanderings. One of their favourite resorts is the unknown land of all horrors lying between the sources of the Pelly and the Hyland.

The rest of our journey up the Frances was uneventful. The ice in the upper cañon was in a dangerous condition, with a wild stream running wherever open water was showing. Here we had to use the utmost caution, testing every step with an axe or pole. Spring ice lets a man through very suddenly, without the moment's warning that

BREAK-UP OF ICE ON THE FRANCES RIVER.

you get in the early winter; and once under the ice in a cañon of a swiftly flowing river you may as well give up all hope at once. Above the cañon we picked up the canoe, and pushed on at our best pace, to reach the lake before the break-up of the ice.

Early on the morning of the 24th of April we came to the outlet of the lake, and made camp while we hauled up the rest of the load from the cache. Two small hand-sleighs were built here, so that we might move our cargo more rapidly over the smooth ice of the lake. Our supplies for the summer now consisted of 200 lbs. of flour, 70 lbs. of bacon, plenty of tea and tobacco, ammunition, fish nets and blankets, and a few clothes, besides picks and shovels, saws, nails, and a little quicksilver in case we should find any of the river bars rich enough in gold to pay us to work with sluice boxes. We had really a very fair supply of provisions if we could kill meat and catch fish as we wanted them, but of course the feeding of our five sleigh-dogs would be a great source of trouble if the game failed us.

Frances Lake was discovered by Robert Campbell in the summer of 1840, and named by him in honour of Lady Simpson, wife of the reigning governor of the Hudson's Bay Company. He established a post at the entrance to the east arm of the lake, and then continued his voyage of discovery to the banks of the Pelly, where, two years later, the trading post known as Pelly Banks was built.

These forts were maintained for about ten years, but the expense and risk of supplying them by the dangerous Liard route was found to be too great, and they were finally abandoned, Fort Frances being occupied till 1851. Since that time the lake has been seldom visited, and has remained the Ultima Thule of the Cassiar miners, few of whom have ever ventured so far; while the crossing to the Pelly was untravelled by white men from Campbell's time till Dr. G. M. Dawson made his Exploratory Survey of the Upper Yukon district in 1887.

The lake should more properly be called a group of lakes, as the two arms, which run nearly parallel to each other for 30 miles, are connected by a narrow channel through which a strong current runs; and again, the upper end of the west arm, a sheet of water forming a basin 5 or 6 miles long, is only reached after passing up a narrow stream a mile in length. The Too-Tsho range of mountains, on the east side of the lake, are rough and broken in the extreme, the Simpson Mountains, to the westward, being more rounded, of less elevation, and altogether more inviting. The long promontory between the two arms is occupied by another high range, with one very conspicuous peak known as Simpson's Tower. The benches which rise from the lake are more thickly wooded than the country we had passed through in ascending the Frances, but in many places the timber has been burnt. Several small streams cut through these benches, and form pretty gravelly points, usually covered with cottonwood and small birch, where they enter the lake. On one of these points, a few miles from the outlet, a man, if he camps quite alone on any summer's night, may, according to the Indians' story, interview the Flying Cariboo, who is sure to perch on a particular dead spruce leaning over the lake. If you treat it kindly, it will occupy its time till sunrise in telling you stories of the old days; but if you are rash enough to shoot at it, it will make things very unpleasant for you. Our Indian guide told us a long yarn explaining how it was that this cariboo was gifted with wings, but Secatz, with the superior knowledge of a man who has lived with the miners and tasted whisky, said it was all nonsense, and would not translate it into the Chinook jargon for our benefit.

The ice on the lake was as yet perfectly sound, except at its outlet and at the mouths of the entering streams, where large stretches of open water were visible. As fresh provisions were rather scarce at this time, we set our nets in some of these places, but could catch no fish, although the lake is known to contain whitefish, trout, and suckers in fair quantities. But in every lake the fishing grounds vary with the seasons, and a stranger may be a long time in hitting off the right place in which to set his net. An appeal to the guide produced the information that he had once caught a good many fish in the summer time in another lake that lay among the Too-Tsho Mountains to the eastward, but he had no suggestion to offer with regard to Frances Lake as a fishing ground in the spring. The moose, too, were unapproachable just when we wanted them, and the cariboo were too far back from the lake to attempt to haul a load of meat to the camp. Even the rabbits and grouse had deserted us, and the wild-fowl had not yet arrived in sufficient numbers to ensure a day's rations. So we had to feed the dogs on bacon and flour that would have been very useful later in the summer, and push on in the hope of killing game at any time.

About 25 miles up the west arm, through which our course lay, the Finlayson River enters from the west side, but being pressed for time, we passed wide of its mouth, and did not put ashore till we reached the upper end of the lake.

The Finlayson was Campbell's route to the Pelly, and Dr. Dawson made his portage by following the same stream; but I hope to discover a shorter portage by continuing up the river that enters at the head of the west arm, thus gaining the advantage of falling on the Pelly at a much higher point than that reached by the old portage, and having at the same time a totally unexplored country to travel through. There is always a special interest in going over ground which is absolutely new, although in Western Canada you know pretty well that it will be merely a repetition of forest, river, and lake, with high mountains in the background, the same old scenery which may be admired as well from the windows of a Pullman car as from the lonely hunting camp on the edge of the Arctic Circle. There is always a vague hope that you may come across a new kind of animal inhabiting a limited area of the vast wilderness, or see the dull glow of a monster nugget shining up through the waters of a creek which lies beyond the utmost limit of the miner's wanderings. That gold exists in the unexplored country to the westward of the northern Rockies can hardly be doubted. Some of the bars on the Porcupine and Liard Rivers, the northern and southern boundaries of this district, have already proved rich in gold, and the eastern tributaries of the Yukon, all, presumably, heading in the same range of mountains, show fair results as far as they have been prospected. There is plenty of ground left for the keen explorer, and a chance of his meeting with a fair reward for his labour.

In the short stretch of running water which has been mentioned before as leading to the extremity of the west arm of Frances Lake, the ice had all disappeared, but the banks were only lightly covered with willow bushes, and a little chopping enabled us to get the sleighs through without trouble. Here we found more wild-fowl than we had yet seen, and killed a few widgeon, teal, and golden-eyes. When we gained the solid ice, and looked over the 6 miles that yet remained to be crossed, we saw a column of smoke rising over the spruce trees, right in our course, but apparently some distance back from the lake shore. On reaching the mouth of the Yus-ez-uh, which enters the north end of the west arm, we were obliged to camp, as the sun was high and the snow melting quickly. Towards evening I sent the two Indians ahead to investigate the cause of the smoke, and try to trade some meat from the encampment they were sure to find. They returned during the night, having met a band of Pelly Indians, who were trapping beaver along the Yus-ez-uh, but they were short of meat themselves and very little inclined to part with any.

The next day I sent the men back to fetch up part of the cargo that we had left half-way down the lake, and went ahead with Secatz, keeping one sleigh to haul up the loads to the Indian camp. The Yus-ez-uh was open in many places, and we had to make several portages entailing much chopping before we reached the camp. Here we found two families, who had left the main band of the Pellys in the autumn and had passed the winter between the Frances and Pelly Lakes, a much finer lot of Indians than any we saw through the Cassiar country, and evidently unspoilt by association with the whites. They were clothed almost entirely in skin garments of their own manufacture, and wore altogether a healthier and more genuine-looking outfit than the Cascas and Liards. None of them were able to speak Chinook, but Secatz could understand them well enough, though he told me there was a marked difference between their language and his own. One of the women wore a large brass ring through her nose—a custom that is rarely practised among interior tribes. It turned out that she had never seen a white man before, as these Indians seldom go into any of the trading posts, and, when they are forced to do so, generally send two of the best travellers ahead with the fur, while the rest of the band remain in the woods, at a long distance from the post, until their return.

A moose had been killed the day before our arrival, so we were able to get a little more meat, though—as usual—we had to pay for it with the

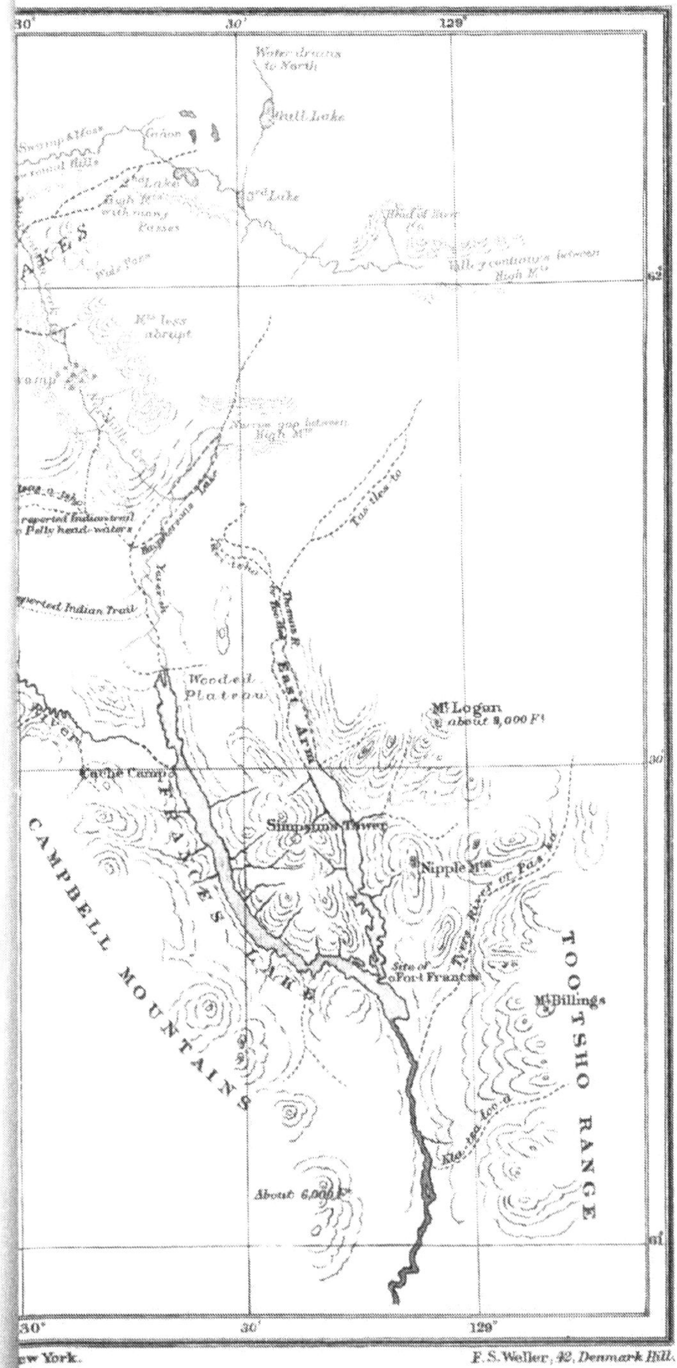

ew York.

F. S. Weller, 42, Denmark Hill.

things we could least afford to do without. But, after all, the savage has reason on his side when he says, that what is most necessary for the white man is very good for the Indian. A black bear had also been seen, but after a long chase with dogs had escaped in the soft snow. It struck me that the first of May was an early date for bears to be out of their winter quarters in such a latitude, but the Indians told me they always see them here when the ice in the Yus-ez-uh begins to break up. The beaver-trapping was going on successfully, and several were brought in during the two or three days that we camped with the Indians. Here we heard an improved version of the story about the cannibals across the divide. They had been on the warpath during the last autumn, and had killed a party of white prospectors far down the Pelly, leaving their bodies stacked up on a gravel bar as a warning to all intruders. As soon as the lakes were open, they intended to bring their canoes across the portage and make a raid on all the white men and Indians whom they met on the Liard and Dease, and had even hopes of plundering the Hudson's Bay Post at Sylvester's Landing.

We had better turn back at once, as we were sure to meet them at the Pelly Lakes, and should have no chance against them. As for trying to reach the source of the Pelly no sane men would attempt such a thing, for even if we were lucky enough to miss the cannibals, the devils in the black cañons among the mountains would quickly put an end to our expedition. However, if we were really determined to go, the Chief of the Indians said he would send a guide with us to show us the main Pelly Lake, but that he should give him strict orders to return at once from there.

The Yus-ez-uh is a fair-sized stream, and, as far as we could judge, easily navigable for a shallow draught boat, with little current at this time of year, winding backwards and forwards across a valley a mile and a half in width, bounded by low round hills which are backed at a considerable distance by mountains, increasing in height and ruggedness as the stream is followed to the northward. The valley itself is a spruce-covered swamp, abounding in small lakes and beaver dams.

CHAPTER IX

PTARMIGAN CREEK

The thaw—Geese and beaver—Macpherson Lake—The divide—Pelly Lake—Wild-fowl—A good place for winter quarters—Running the canoe down Ptarmigan Creek.

As soon as all the cargo was up, we pushed on again, taking an Indian named Narchilla as guide. Our first guide, who had joined us at the mouth of the Frances, continued with us, as, although he admitted frankly that he knew nothing of the country, he was useful for hauling a hand-sleigh, and would be a companion for Secatz in his journey back to the Liard Post. We found the travelling difficult enough after leaving the Indians' encampment, as the hours of frost were rapidly getting shorter and the ice was becoming more rotten each day. Men and sleighs were continually breaking through, to the great detriment of our tea and other perishable articles, but the weather was warm and wood plentiful, so the men were nothing the worse for an occasional mishap. The snow was going off quickly, and it seemed doubtful whether there would be enough left on the portage to take us across the divide. We could only make 7 or 8 miles a day at our best speed, and after three days' struggling up the river, we were stopped about 20 miles from the mouth by a continuous stretch of open water. Here we put ashore to patch up the canoe, which had opened out in the seams during the long journey on the sleigh, but a little caulking with oakum and pitch, and a rough coat of paint, made her as tight as ever in a couple of days. We then loaded her up, and, sending the dogs overland with the empty sleighs, paddled 3 miles up stream to a small lake that lay in the course of the river, from which point we were to begin the portage towards the Pelly.

During this time, although the travelling had been hard, we fared much better in the matter of provisions, as the geese were turning up in some numbers. Beaver, too, were remarkably plentiful, more so than I ever remember seeing them in any part of Canada. You may find a country where there is every sign of beaver, where they have chopped down numbers of big trees, and the size of their dams shows that there must be plenty of workers, but they are seldom visible. But at the head of the Yus-ez-uh, on any fine evening, we could paddle along quietly in the canoe, and get two or three shots at them sitting motionless on the ice that still clung to the banks. Their fur and meat are at their best, too, in the spring, and, when Secatz killed a large bull moose close to the edge of the little lake, and many fat geese were brought into the camp, there was a time of plenty and general contentment for men and dogs. Our failure to kill moose for such a length of time had seriously crippled us in the matter of provisions, and the last two weeks had played havoc with our flour and bacon.

At this camp the first rain of the year fell on 9th May, a heavy storm lasting all night, and washing away most of the snow. A sharp frost set in, however, as soon as the rain ceased, and formed a good crust, which helped us greatly during the next few days.

As we stopped for a day at the lake, while the Indians were making the road on the first part of the portage, I made a short expedition to try if I could find Macpherson Lake, which was known to lie at the head of the Yus-ez-uh, and after walking 5 miles, sometimes on the bank, sometimes on the ice, and sometimes up the bed of the stream—which here becomes shallow and easily waded in many places—I had the satisfaction of reaching the lake. It is said by Henry Thibert, who visited it some years ago, to be 10 miles in length, but I could get no view of the far end, as the lake bends to the north-eastward about 4 miles from the outlet, and the ice was so deeply submerged by the melting snow that I could not wade out far enough to see round the intervening point. The lake is characterised by the same terrace-like formation of the forested-plateau which distinguishes Frances Lake; but the high mountains approach much more closely to the water, and, as seen from a distance, the valley at the head of the lake seems to be little more than a narrow gorge between rough peaks of great elevation. There was a large patch of open water close to the outlet, and here wild-fowl were in great abundance—mallard, widgeon, pintail, teal, and golden-eyes being the most plentiful varieties.

I saw several otters, too, and they must be increasing in number rapidly in this part of the country, as very few of the Indians will touch them, although their skins fetch a good price from the fur-traders. A curious superstition prevails that if you kill an otter it is capable of causing much trouble by coming to life again in your stomach. Only three winters ago a Frances Lake woman lay at death's door with this malady, but she was saved by the timely arrival of the only medicine man left in the tribe. He seems to have diagnosed the case correctly at once, and holding a sheep's horn spoon to the patient's mouth, he proceeded to repeat a long incantation suitable to the occasion. As soon as he had finished, to the great joy of all the relations who had gathered to see the death, three little otters dropped out into the spoon. The old lady recovered rapidly, and afterwards confessed to having stolen and eaten an otter that she had found in somebody else's beaver trap during a long period of starvation in the early summer.

A large tributary joins the Yus-ez-uh from the westward just below the lake, and at its head a lake, Ustus-a-tsho, is marked on Dr. Dawson's map in dotted lines, from Indian report furnished him by Thibert; but although we followed this stream in the course of our portage to its very source, we found no lake, and our guide, Narchilla, knew nothing of any sheet of water bearing that name. There are two large streams entering the Yus-ez-uh from the same side, at some distance lower down, one within a few miles of its mouth, and it is quite likely that the lake in question is situated on one of these tributaries.

Our rate of travelling when we struck into the woods on the portage was still slow, as we had to make double trips with the loads, which had till lately been much lighter from the pressure of hard times, but were now increased by the weight of the moose meat. Our guide followed the south bank of the stream that I have mentioned as flowing towards Macpherson Lake, through a rolling country timbered with a thick growth of spruce that had been burnt before it had attained any great size. The actual valley of the creek—which we called Narchilla Creek for want of a better name—is extremely rough, following closely the base of a high, broken range of mountains, which appear to be a western spur of the Too-Tsho range, and, according to our pilot, contain no game of any kind. The southern side of the pass, which here lies nearly east and west, presents a much more pleasing appearance. The undulating plateau is clothed with scattered bunches of spruce and black pine, and rises gently to the summits of grassy, bare-topped mountains, already clear of snow in patches.

About 18 miles from the little lake we reached a large swamp, which forms the watershed of the streams that find their way to the mouth of the Mackenzie by the Frances and Liard, and those that reach the Behring Sea at the mouth of the Yukon. At the far end of the swamp the water was running to the westward, and after passing through two small lakes, and being increased by the junction of two or three little streams, had developed into a good-sized creek, within 6 miles of the summit. We named it Ptarmigan Creek, from the number of these birds that we found in the swamp at its head. The pass here turns more to the northward and continues in that direction for 16 miles by our reckoning, to the shore of the Pelly Lake. The mountains on each side become less connected, with many wide passes through which small streams drain into Ptarmigan Creek.

But although the distance was short, we failed in our attempt to get the sleighs through to the lake, as on the far side of the divide we found the snow had almost entirely disappeared. Large grassy swamps covered with willow brush took the place of the heavy spruce growth, and in these swamps the sun had been able to exert its full power on the snow, and the ground was bare. The consequence was that we had to camp on the bank of Ptarmigan Creek, within about 5 miles of the lake in a straight line, to await the breaking up of the ice, when we hoped to run down with the canoe to the lake if the creek should prove navigable.

And here our three Indians turned back, Narchilla having approached near enough the haunts of the bad men. Secatz, too, who had really done very well in coming so far into a strange country, was much impressed with his danger, and made a final appeal to me to abandon the expedition, but, finding it of no avail, cautioned us to be on our guard with any Indians we might meet, and taking with him as much ammunition and tobacco as we would give him, started back for the camp on the Yus-ez-uh,

PELLY LAKE.

where he hoped to be able to borrow a canoe to run down the Frances and Liard to the Lower Post. They all reached their destinations in safety, and thoroughly alarmed their friends with the story of the intended raid that was to be made on them by the Pellys in the summer.

On 16th May, after stowing our cargo on a high scaffold above the reach of the wolverines and of the floods that usually follow the first movement of the ice, we started on foot for the lake, each man and dog carrying a light load. Snow-shoes were thrown away here, as the ground was bare in most places, and the snow that remained in the drifts was too soft to be of any service. We found no signs of a trail, although Narchilla had told us that there was a well-marked path used by the Indians in summer, so we forced our way through the willow scrub, and waded swamps and small creeks, till at last we reached the smooth gravelly beach on the south shore of the main Pelly Lake and made camp at the mouth of Ptarmigan Creek. Our first move, as usual, was to try what means of subsistence the lake was likely to afford, and we went to work at once to build a raft from which to set a net in the open water at the mouth of the creek. The ice was already showing signs of breaking up, and a narrow channel had formed all round the weather shore of the lake, while the deep water ice, though still strong enough to travel on, was honeycombed with small holes, and the whole mass moved with every shift of wind.

Subsequent exploration proved that the main Pelly Lake is a crescent-shaped sheet of water some 8 miles in length, and perhaps 2 in width, lying in a general north-east and south-west direction. The east end of the lake is bordered by low conical hills alternating with swamps, the whole country being covered with a light growth of spruce, tamarac, and willow, nowhere of sufficient density to be an impediment to travel. At the west end, a high range of grassy mountains rises nearly straight from the shore of the south side, and immediately opposite stands a single rocky pinnacle, forming a conspicuous landmark for any one approaching the lake from below by way of the Pelly, which enters at the extreme east end and finds its outlet at the extreme west end of the lake. Of the other entering streams Ptarmigan Creek is by far the largest, none of the others being of any importance, although swollen by melting snow to their utmost capacity at the time of our visit. The mouths of these incoming creeks are all marked by the same gravelly points that are so noticeable on Frances Lake, affording excellent landing-places for any canoe that has to put ashore through stress of weather.

As soon as the net was in the water I set off across the ice to explore the mouth of the Upper Pelly, which lay about a mile away from the camp, and was disappointed to find it a much smaller stream than it was supposed to be from the account of it given to Campbell by Indians at the time of the existence of the Pelly Banks Post. It was wide enough, and apparently deep near its mouth, but there was no current perceptible, and its valley, which was here a couple of miles in width, contracted rapidly and appeared to be little better than a narrow cañon at a distance of 10 miles up stream. The swamps and small lakes that lay near the mouth of the river were occupied as a breeding-ground by an abundance of wild-fowl. Geese, mallard, widgeon, teal, pintail, scaups, golden-eyes, long-tailed and harlequin ducks, scoters, great wathern, black and red throated divers, gulls, and terns, were all in plenty, with a few swans and many other varieties in less numbers. The common snipe of America (*Scopolax Wilsonii*) was drumming overhead, and sandpipers and phalaropes kept up a continual screaming in the marches.

The fishing ground at Ptarmigan Creek turned out to be no good, but fortunately we discovered two small dug-out canoes at an old Indian camp near the head of the lake, and, as there was enough open water round the edge of the ice for a canoe to pass, we shifted camp to the mouth of the Pelly, to be nearer the goose hunting-ground in case the fishing proved a total failure. This seemed likely enough to happen, as we caught almost nothing till, on the fourth day of our stay at the lake, after shifting the nets half a dozen times, we hit upon a paying spot at the mouth of a large slough, a couple of miles up the Pelly. Here we caught a dozen white-fish and suckers before we had done setting the net, and afterwards had no difficulty in keeping up the fish supply, which was varied by a few jack and occasionally a large trout. We at once built a drying stage, on which to smoke any fish that we could not eat, with the aid of the dogs, so as to have a stock in hand to fall back upon if any scarcity of provisions should arise during the journey we intended to make to the source of the river.

The Pelly Lake would be a remarkably good

point at which to winter for anybody who had reason for so doing. Besides the fish I have mentioned, the salmon run up to the lake in great numbers in the autumn, and, though they must be in poor condition after their journey of over 2000 miles from the Behring Sea, they would be useful enough for dog-feed. Then, a little to the westward, there is a good cariboo mountain, and the moose are everywhere, so there should be little risk of starvation if the wintering party were properly equipped with fishing gear and ammunition.

When we thought the ice had broken up in Ptarmigan Creek, I went back with Smith and Alick to the place where we had cached the canoe, leaving Archie to go on with the fish-drying and look after the dogs while we were away. A day was spent in pitching the canoe and dividing up the cargo, as the wild appearance of the creek made it too risky to hazard the whole load. On 21st May, late in the afternoon, we started to run down to the lake, without any knowledge of the stream we were going to navigate. We had made some ineffectual attempts to examine its course from the banks at different times, but the timber was so thick close to the water that we could see very little. We knew, however, that there were some rapids to be run, as we could hear their roar in the distance while we were walking to and from the lake.

The creek was much swollen by the melting snow, and a strong current swept us round the first few stretches of easy water in safety, but below this the reaches were so short that we could never see any distance ahead, and we had to use every precaution to keep clear of drift piles and the overhanging ice which still lined the banks in several places. The current always seemed to set right on to these spots, where, besides the probability of the canoe being capsized if she ran under the hanging mass, there was always a chance of the ice falling on our heads and bringing us to utter grief. Sometimes a log had fallen across the stream, and a delay was caused by chopping out a channel. Only once we had to portage—over a drift pile which completely choked the creek for a distance of 300 yards. Below this, the rapids began, none of them very formidable, but with scattered boulders lying right across the stream, which kept winding backwards and forwards from one side of the valley to the other, and only getting a mile ahead after running three or four times that distance out of its course. At several corners we used a line, and dropped the canoe down carefully. At others, we turned her head up stream, and, keeping good steerage way with the paddles, dodged down stern first among the rocks and snags. We camped before reaching the lake, as a snow-storm increased the little darkness after sunset, and it was hard enough to keep clear of the various obstructions even in good daylight. The next morning brought a repetition of sudden alarms and narrow shaves, but at eight o'clock we ran the last rapid and shot out into the quiet water of the lake without even a scratch on the canoe. During the whole of the long journey we made in the summer with this canoe, although we ran some big rapids, and had to face some bad weather on the Lower Yukon, and afterwards on the Behring Sea, we never encountered a stretch of water that tested our capabilities as canoe men so much as the first short run of fifteen or twenty miles down the Ptarmigan Creek.

CHAPTER X

EXPEDITION TOWARDS SOURCE OF PELLY RIVER

Disease among the rabbits—Swallows' nests—Drying fish—Upper Pelly Lake —Gull Lake—Ptarmigans nesting and signs of summer—Accident to rifle —A bad miss—Dogs go astray; their instinct.

AT the fish camp Archie had been doing pretty well with the nets, and thinking we had enough fish to start with, we set out on the following day to examine the source of the Pelly, taking with us, in addition to our own canoe, one of the little dug-outs that we took the liberty of borrowing from the old Indian camp. She was exceedingly useful as a hunting canoe, as I could paddle or pole her up stream quickly and quietly while the men were bringing up the big canoe with more difficulty and more noise, owing to her greater draught of water when loaded. I had thus many good opportunities for sneaking up on the geese, which at this time formed our principal food-supply. They were all the big Canada geese; not in the great numbers that we afterwards saw on the tundra, near the mouth of the Yukon, but enough always to provide us with a living. There were more rabbits too than we had seen for a long time, but they had turned brown and were not in such good condition as they had been before the snow went off. Many of them too were covered externally and internally with the ulcers which form the first stage of the peculiar disease which, at regularly recurring periods, exterminates nearly every rabbit in the country.

By this time spring had fairly set in, the buds were breaking on the willow bushes, and a few flowers were in bloom on the river banks. The first goose's nest was found on 24th May, and the eggs promptly devoured.

For about 15 miles the river wound leisurely in and out through the swamps, but then the valley contracted suddenly, the banks became high and gravelly, and the current much increased in force, with frequent little rapids. An evening's prospecting on a gravel bar produced a few colours of gold, but there was no indication that any of the bars would pay to work. Twenty-five miles up from the lake, following the course of the river, but probably not more than half that distance in a straight line, we reached what was evidently the head of navigation. The stream here makes a sharp bend to the eastward, and enters a cañon that forbids the passage of a canoe. On the south side of the river a colony of swallows had taken possession of a bluff, their nests forming a very curious sight. A description of these swallows (*Petrochelidon Pyrrhonota*) is to be found in Messrs. Sharpe and Wyatt's interesting monograph on swallows. On the Lower Yukon, where civilisation has advanced, these birds are very quick to accept the hospitality offered them, and have entirely deserted their inconvenient nesting-places on the river bluffs for the shelter of the eaves of the miners' cabins. I walked ahead to inspect the river, crossing a range of low conical hills, and thus cutting across the bend came out on the bank above the cañon. But here the volume of water was so small, and the rapids so frequent, that it did not seem worth while to attempt to force our way up with the canoe any further. I discovered, however, a small lake lying in the course of the stream, and the idea at once suggested itself that, if we could catch fish in this lake,

SWALLOW BLUFF.

it would be a good place for present headquarters, and afford an excellent starting-point for a journey on foot to the head of the river. I had a shot at a moose on the edge of the lake, but he got away from me and we did not find his carcass until several days afterwards, when, of course, the meat was spoilt except for dog food.

Leaving the big canoe and everything not absolutely necessary at the foot of the cañon, Alick and I packed the dogs with as much as they could carry, and went overland to the lake, to wait the arrival of Smith and Archie, who undertook to carry the little dug-out across the cañon, and bring her up to the lake by water. This they found harder work than they expected, and Archie, who was always a little timid in strong water, had some bad frights as Smith made him get into the canoe and steer her through the rapids wherever it was possible to use a tracking line. It seems that they had some very narrow shaves, and two days were occupied in making the journey, but the labour was not wasted, as the dug-out proved invaluable for tending the nets and hunting ducks during our stay at the lake.

This sheet of water is probably the one marked

on some of the maps, from Indian report, as the upper of the two Pelly Lakes, but it is of such insignificant size that the Indians would have been hardly likely to make mention of it, unless it had the reputation of being a good fishing-ground, which we certainly found it to be. It is a curiously shaped little lake, consisting of two round basins, each half a mile in length, connected by a narrow, canal-like passage about the same length. The river does not pass through the lake, but just touches the north side of the western basin and leaves it immediately. The shores are everywhere swampy, but rise at once into low irregular hills covered with willow scrub, which here seems to have entirely taken the place of the spruce timber.

When the nets were set, and the pile of fish on the drying stages was increasing rapidly, I did a little exploration of the surrounding country. About 5 miles to the eastward I found that the river came through another little lake, and afterwards turned to the south-east. Leaving the main stream, I followed up a small tributary, coming in through a wide pass from the north, and soon crossed a swampy divide, on the far side of which was a creek, running to the north. Another

5 miles brought me to a lake about 4 miles in length, which I called Gull Lake, from the numbers of black-headed gulls that had selected it for a breeding-ground. I camped for the night at the end of this lake, levying tribute on the gulls' nests for supper and breakfast, and intended to follow down a good-sized creek that was flowing through a broad valley towards the north, but in the morning it was alternately raining and snowing so hard that I turned back for the fish lake. I was sorry afterwards that I did not go on a few miles farther. At the time, I thought the creek would most probably bend to the westward and join a tributary of the Pelly, the mouth of which we had noticed just below the cañon, although the volume of water leaving the lake seemed rather too great to be accounted for in this manner. Judging by the light of our later discovery (made after we had passed through the Pelly Lakes on our down-stream journey) of a large river heading to the north-eastward—and really entitled to be called the main stream of the Pelly—I have little doubt that if I had followed down the creek draining Gull Lake I should have reached the bank of this river at a point perhaps 50 miles farther up stream than its

junction with the river running through the Pelly Lakes. The rain poured down in torrents for a couple of days, accompanied by thunder and lightning, interfering with our fish-drying operations, and preventing our start for the head of the river, but on 5th June we were able to break camp, and started with heavy loads for men and dogs in a south-easterly direction, reaching the bank of the river again after a straight cut of five or six miles.

The thick willow scrub, with which the country is covered, interfered greatly with the rate of travel, making especially hard work for the dogs to get their bulky side-packs between the bushes. They required constant watching, too, as they soon discovered that the easiest method of lightening their loads was to devour the dried fish they were carrying, and we sometimes found all the dogs playing havoc with a pack that had slipped off in forcing through the bushes.

The river had now become very narrow, and was little better than a succession of rapids, quite unfit for navigation by even a small canoe. The valley, running south-east by south, is here about two miles in width, bounded by detached mountains, separated by broad passes, and increasing in height towards the head of the valley, which continues in the same direction, although the river makes a sharp bend to the eastward about 20 miles in a straight line from our fish lake, and then heads back, with a sharp rise, to the north, winding from side to side of a swampy gorge less than a mile in width. At the head of this cul-de-sac, three torrents of melting snow collect their waters and form what we supposed at the time to be the source of the Pelly. This was rather a disappointing finish to our expedition, as we had expected to find the Pelly a larger stream heading in a more northerly direction, and had even some hopes of crossing the divide at its head and making an attempt to reach the Mackenzie by some stream flowing to the eastward. But the distance we had come by the river we had followed was so short, and in such an unsatisfactory direction, that we could not yet be very far away from Macpherson Lake, and, if we crossed the range of mountains ahead of us, we should only find the water draining into Hyland River at the best, and more probably into the Frances. We camped at the head of the gorge in a patch of dwarf spruce, where ptarmigan were in great numbers and afforded us an easy way of making a living. Our fish supply was nearly at an end, as we had been several days on the way, and a good many of the fish were lost or eaten by the dogs. Alick had missed the only moose that had been seen, although there were a good many tracks; but we did very little hunting, as a moose is almost too big to handle when travelling on foot—either most of the meat is wasted, or a delay is caused by camping close to the carcass until it is finished, so it is really better to kill small game as required for the day's rations. The first ptarmigan's nest, containing five fresh eggs, was found on 10th June, close to the camp; in fact there were nests all round us, these birds seeming almost gregarious in their breeding habits at this particular spot. It was a place very suitable for their purpose, a steep side hill exposed to the full power of the sun, covered with a thick, low growth of willow and stunted spruce, the latter spreading out into a dense trailing bush within a couple of feet of the ground. The birds were, of course, in full summer plumage, looking their very best, and it seemed a great pity to have to kill any of them. They had no fear of us, and as soon as we turned into our blankets they pitched on the little bushes all round the camp and discussed the strange invasion with evident disapproval. The long laughing chuckle of the cock ptarmigan—a very different note to his poor little winter gurgle—is as suggestive of the coming of summer in the Canadian North as the cry of the cuckoo in an English copse. It may be heard in the first warm days of May, and speaks at once of running water loosed from the grasp of winter, of the green moss showing up in patches through the melting snow, and the little buds shooting on birch and willow. A few pairs of black-headed gulls were breeding down in the swamp, and small birds were much more abundant than one would suppose at this elevation and in such a northerly latitude. Among them were the Canadian robin and blackbird, apparently happy enough, but looking rather out of place among the ptarmigan and the snow that was still lying on the ground in patches. Vegetation, of course, was much later at this altitude than we had left it at the fish lake, where the willows were already in leaf; here the buds were only just formed, and no flowers were visible, although several varieties were in full bloom along the banks of the lower river.

And now an accident happened that would have

been trivial enough if it had taken place in civilisation, but very serious on an expedition of this kind. I had been to the top of a small mountain to collect some geological specimens, and get what view I could of the surrounding country, and reached the camp just in time to see Alick throw a large stick of firewood down on my Winchester rifle, which I had left with him to shoot ptarmigan for supper. The stock was broken and some of the inside mechanism bent so badly that, without any tools, it was hardly possible to repair the damage. We pulled it to pieces and patched it up as well as we could, with the unsatisfactory result that it would go off occasionally, but averaged three miss-fires to every shot—a most unreliable weapon for a man to depend upon when the rifle is his bread-winner. Smith had a small ·44 Winchester, and I still had a Paradox with a very few ball cartridges, but the unserviceable condition of my long range rifle was afterwards the cause of our hurried journey down the Pelly below the lakes, where I should like to have spent a month or two in exploring the heads of some of the tributary streams coming in from a range of mountains to the westward of the river. As there seemed to be no object in continuing our journey to the westward, we turned back downstream and reached the fish lake after ten days' absence, found it as reliable as ever, catching twenty-five fish the same night. Among them was a giant white-fish, weighing at least twelve pounds, though the men all put it down as over twenty pounds—a remarkable fish to come out of such a small lake. The Indians whom we met at the head of Frances Lake had told us of a fish they sometimes catch in the Pelly Lake, resembling the white-fish, but which they call the "Salmon's Cousin," on account of its size. The ordinary white-fish seldom exceeds five or six pounds in any lake, but there is little doubt as to the identity of this specimen, as I have seen white-fish in many different parts of Canada, and my crew were all Manitoba men who had worked at the fisheries on Lake Winnipeg.

The overland portage and the inevitable pitching of the canoe occupied a couple of days, and then we started on our long down-stream journey. The water was higher than when we came up, and most of the rocks were covered, so that we had no difficulty in running all the little rapids. A few miles down, a moose jumped into the water and crossed the river just in front of the canoe. In some unaccountable manner, the bowsman missed it altogether, though it gave him an easy enough chance. I tried a shot from the stern, as we were badly in need of meat, and if we could kill a moose now none would be wasted, but a miss-fire was the only result, and our promised feast went crashing through the willows. It is a good rule in a canoe to let the bowsman do all the shooting, and it is only in cases of emergency, or in still water, that the sternsman should hazard a shot, unless it is at an animal that appears behind the canoe, when there is no time to swing the bow round. There is usually plenty of work in looking after the safety of the canoe in swift-running water, without taking the risk of blowing the next man's head off if a swirl of the current happens to bring it in line with the animal you mean to shoot.

During the excitement caused by the moose, all the dogs disappeared, but, thinking they would find their way down to the old camp, we did not waste much time in waiting for them, though we had afterwards a good deal of trouble to hunt them up. Everybody was rather gloomy at the loss of the expected meat feast, but a few geese were killed lower down, and the lake looked so pleasant, now that the ice had gone and the deciduous trees were all in leaf, that even the unlucky individual who had missed the moose recovered his spirits before we reached our old camping-ground at the mouth of Ptarmigan Creek. As we still had part of our cargo stowed away at the place where we had first launched the canoe—5 miles up the creek—I sent the men to bring it down, while I made an expedition to the foot of the lake in the dug-out, to find the outlet of the river, and see if there were any Indians in the neighbourhood. My passage along the lake was interrupted by thunderstorms, with violent wind-squalls, and as my little canoe was hardly seaworthy, I had several times to run for the shore and wait for a more favourable chance. On reaching the outlet I passed into a swift-running stream, and within half a mile found myself at the head of a rapid. Here I landed to pick out a course, and discovered another lake just ahead. The dug-out ran gaily down through the broken water, and I crossed a round lake a mile and a half in width. After another short stretch of current with another rapid, I came to a narrow sheet of water 3 miles in length, and camped at its western extremity. An evening's moose hunt produced nothing, but from the top of a small hill I had an excellent view of the valley ahead, stretching away in a south-westerly direction through a flat, forested country, broken only in one spot by an isolated group of bare-topped mountains.

The shores of these small lakes are everywhere swampy, and thick moss covers the ground between the stunted spruce and the tamarac. In the stretches of river between the lakes the banks are in places high and gravelly, and most of the timber has been burnt recently, but I could see no signs of Indians having been here since the previous autumn.

In the course of these long expeditions, made in company with half-breeds, it is always a relief to get away by yourself for a night or two, especially in the summer, when there is no trouble about the cold, and you can lie down anywhere without digging out the snow and cutting a supply of pine brush and firewood. The endless chatter of the half-breeds, good fellows enough though they may be for their work, becomes tiresome when you have once heard all their self-glorifying stories and the performances of the various dogs they have driven at different times of their lives. It is always the same indefinite yarn about some long day's journey they once made, the time at which they left camp, the number of halts they made to boil the kettle, and the time of arrival at the next camp, after travelling an unmeasured distance. Or else they discuss the valiant deeds of some half-breed bruiser of Manitoba, and the punching of heads which seems greatly in fashion along the Red River on New Year's Day and other festive occasions. A pleasant change from this is the quiet camp all to yourself, with your little canoe hauled up on the shore of a peaceful lake, where the cries of the wild birds and animals seem far more in keeping with the surroundings than the guffaws of a crowd of tobacco-chewing half-breeds, lacking both the decency of the white man and the dignified reserve which still marks the true bred native of the Northern forest.

I reached the main camp late on the following evening, after making a risky crossing of the lake, to learn that the men had found the cache untouched, and had brought down half the load, but that no fish were to be caught at the mouth of Ptarmigan Creek, and that the dogs had not yet come in from the Upper Pelly, where we had abandoned them three days before. The next morning the men made another journey to the cache, with orders to bring down everything, and I paddled back up-stream to hunt up the dogs. I found two of them sitting gloomily in our old camp at the fish slough, a couple of miles from the head of the lake. They looked very wretched as, besides being lean and hungry, they had been rending each other, and the flies had irritated the sore places till the dogs were nearly crazy. The other two were not so easily found, and it was not till I had nearly reached the head of navigation, and the sun was long down, that I heard a dog howling in the woods. He came to the sound of a rifle-shot, but was in a worse condition than the others, and refused to move any further till I had given him a duck and a white-fish to cheer him up. The canoe was so small that he would be nearly certain to capsize it if he came on board, so I drifted down slowly and made him run through the brush along the bank, after I had hunted a couple of hours for the fourth missing dog and finally given him up as lost for ever.

It is worthy of record, as an example of what the faculty we call instinct can accomplish, that this other dog turned up at the Lower Post on the

Liard, very thin, and with his nose and mouth full of porcupine quills, late in the following October, having not only found his way, but also hunted his food, for a distance of 250 miles, and this, too, without the advantage of his back track to follow, as we had come up on the ice, which had all disappeared before the dog was lost.

CHAPTER XI

DOWN THE PELLY RIVER

Salmon a long distance from the sea—Claims of Pelly River to be considered main branch of Yukon—Scarcity of provisions—A cow moose—Slate Rapid—Hoole River—A grizzly bear and the result of a broken rifle.

I REACHED the camp at sunrise, and, after hauling up the dug-out in a shady spot to keep her from cracking, we loaded up the canoe and started along the lake, with the dogs running on the beach, to continue our voyage down the Pelly. In the third lake we tried the nets off the point of a little island —the only island, by the way, in any of these lakes —but again without success. On the following day we passed out of the lakes and found the river running, with a good current, between low, gravelly banks, bearing many signs of old Indian encampments. The huge stages for drying fish, and the traps carefully stowed away for future use, suggested great abundance of salmon in the autumn, while the skeletons of these fish were to be seen everywhere scattered along the banks of the little creeks. Every year, no doubt, the Pelly Indians camp here to gather their harvest, which needs no sowing, but comes of its own accord from the distant waters of the Behring Sea. I have never heard any satisfactory explanation as to the reasons some of the salmon have for pushing on to the very head of a stream, when spawning grounds seemingly of equal attraction are to be found close to the sea up any of the tributaries. Why, for instance, do some of the Yukon fish turn up the first stream flowing in from the tundra, and others run up the main river 2300 miles to the Pelly Lakes? And what a river it is, to afford such a long run without a waterfall to stop the passage of a fish!

The country is here very level, and heavily wooded with spruce of larger growth than we had seen round the lakes, interspersed with a plentiful supply of small cottonwood.

After following down the stream for about 8 miles in a general south-west direction, although with many turns on the course of the stream, we were suddenly surprised, on rounding a bend, by running into a big broad river heading a little to the eastward of north, with a strong current swollen by the melting snows — fully three times the size of the stream that we had been following with the mistaken idea that we were exploring the source of the Pelly, whereas we had in reality only succeeded in reaching the head of a comparatively small tributary. We put ashore at once and stretched the nets across the mouth of a small slough, where we hoped to replenish our supply of provisions, which was now very scanty. Our flour and bacon were practically finished, and the nets and rifles had produced hardly anything lately, so that there seemed to be some danger of a period of starvation setting in—and this, too, when we had a chance to explore a river unknown to any white man, and unmarked in any map, heading away towards the distant range of high snow-capped mountains that were just visible from our camp. This must be the river which the Indians speak of when they tell their stories of the evil spirits that live in the black cañons among the mountains, as the natural features of the stream running through the lakes are rather tame, and not at all likely to give foundation to romance. Secatz must have heard of this river from the Indians at Frances Lake, but either thought it was not worth while mentioning to us, or else considered it better for our own safety that we should know nothing about it.

The high stage of the water, which was still rising, seemed to indicate that the river must have its source in mountains of great altitude, and at a considerable distance from where we first saw it, as by this time—20th June—the stream draining the lakes had fallen several feet, and the mountains near its head had been nearly bare of snow a fortnight before. It is probable, therefore, that when the main stream of the Pelly is explored, it will be found to head directly on the western slope of the Rocky Mountains, perhaps offering an easy route to one of the small streams falling into the Mackenzie between Fort Simpson and Fort Norman. This addition to the total length of the Pelly, which has always been calculated from the supposed position of the lakes, will help to prove that river's claim to be considered the main branch of the Yukon, although the Lewes, which joins the Pelly at Fort Selkirk, has usually been looked upon as the more important stream of the two.

It soon became evident that we could make no use of the discovery we had made—our chance was missed when we turned up stream from the main Pelly Lake. If we had known anything about this stream, and had reached the spot at which we were now camped in the middle of May, we should have had a fortnight's low water just after the break-up of the ice, besides a sufficient supply of provisions to enable us to push on quickly while the bars were uncovered and the current slack. In that time we might have penetrated a long way into a totally unexplored country, and have reached the source of a really important river, instead of wasting our time in exploring a miserable little stream that led to nothing. But now, apart from the provision question, it was almost impossible to travel up stream. The water was running high among the willows that fringe the banks, a savage current was bringing down huge rafts of drift logs, and all the numerous difficulties presented by a large river in flood-time were fully developed.

The nets caught a few fish during the two days we waited to see if the water would fall, but hardly enough for our immediate use, and there was no prospect of a supply of dried fish to lay by for emergencies. Moose-hunting was again a failure, and, as frequently happens, the geese and ducks all disappeared when there was most need of them. The periods of good and bad times are always very distinctly marked when the rifle and net are depended upon entirely for the supply of provisions. No matter how good a hunter or fisherman you may be, there are sure to be spells of scanty living if none of the party have any local knowledge as to the best places for game or fish, and you often come across a strip of country entirely deserted by birds and beasts. Fishing in a large river during high water is seldom satisfactory, as a net can only be set in some quiet backwater to be clear of the strong current and drifting logs; and such places are not always to be found.

On the third day I reluctantly gave orders to proceed down stream, as we had several hundred miles to go before we could reach any of the trading posts on the Yukon, and the first part of the distance was through an unknown country, where we might encounter bad rapids and long portages enough to cause a delay that would be serious, unless we had better luck in our hunting.

At first our course lay through the same flat,

mossy country, but gradually the banks rose in height, and became first gravelly, and then took the form of high bluffs composed of several different kinds of rock or sand, alternated with stretches of low-lying banks on both sides of the river. About 20 miles down we put ashore to wash a panful of dirt at the mouth of a wide shallow stream coming in on the north side, but two or three colours of gold were the only results.

Just below this the current in the river increased in strength, and we soon heard the roar of a rapid ahead. On landing to inspect the danger, we found rather a wild stretch of water, with many scattered rocks at its head, and a very heavy sea at the lower end of the rapid, where the river is confined to a narrow cañon-like constriction between low slate bluffs. There was an intricate although quite practicable channel among the rocks, but no convenient eddy into which to drop to avoid the heavy sea, so that if we once started we had to run the whole rapid.

Unless in the case of a perfectly straight piece of water, when you can form a pretty good opinion of the danger by standing up in the stern of the canoe, it is always well to put ashore, and take a look at what lies ahead, when travelling down an unknown stream, as you may find yourself at the brink of a cascade, or an utterly impassable rapid, when it is too late to make a landing. Don't listen to the valiant fool in the bow, who shouts: "Oh, hell! we can run that!" just as you are shooting into the eddy; and if he tries to enforce his opinion by dragging the bow of the canoe out into the current, no experienced voyageur will blame you for clubbing him on the head with pole or paddle. He cannot know anything more about what is round the corner than you do, if he has never seen the place before.

It is pleasant enough to play about in the rapids in a light canoe when civilisation is close at hand and the loss caused by a capsize or collision with a rock can be easily replaced; but when the accident happens 500 miles from the nearest trading-post the possible result of a mistake is serious enough to make the most reckless steersman reflect a little before he plunges his canoe into the swirling waters. If anything goes wrong it is a case of total shipwreck, and the men who reach the bank in safety are really little better off than those who come to sudden grief among the rocks. Everything is gone.

There are no matches that would light a fire to dry the soaking clothes; no axe to build a raft with; nothing to eat; no rifle, ammunition, or fish-hooks with which to kill game or fish that would provide a means of subsistence to a properly equipped party. The only means of progression is a misshapen ungovernable raft of drift timber bound together with willow twigs and turned loose down stream till it flies to pieces on the first rock, or drifts under an overhanging log-jam, each accident being likely to further reduce the number of the crew.

On this occasion, however, none of these unpleasant things happened; and by dropping the canoe down carefully with a line from point to point, and making an easy portage of a quarter of a mile on the north side of the river, we avoided all the danger, and camped at the foot of the rapid. Leaving the men to carry over the cargo, I went for an evening's moose-hunt, and, finding a fresh track, was lucky enough to come across a big cow moose stripping the willow-bushes for her evening feed on the edge of a small muddy lake. It was an awkward spot for a stalk, but, after a long detour, I managed to creep into a bunch of willows towards which she was heading. There I lay in a pool of water for an hour at the mercy of the mosquitoes, which are particularly bad along the Upper Pelly; and knowing that, if the moose came within shot, there was an even chance of a miss-fire from my broken rifle, to say nothing of the possibility of missing or lightly wounding the animal; and that, if I did not kill, there would be little supper in camp that night, as we had absolutely nothing left but a few pounds of flour that we had been using with great care. But everything went well; the moose came straight towards me, and finally stood broadside at fifty yards. The rifle went off at the first pull, and a death-shot was the result. I snapped the next cartridge three times in succession as the moose ran into the lake. But it made no difference, as she turned over and lay floating among a bunch of yellow water-lilies within ten yards of the shore. She was much too heavy for me to handle alone in the deep water, so I went back to camp at once to get the men to give me a hand. We hauled her out with a line, and little pieces of meat were cooking on sticks over a fire before the skin was fairly off the animal. The sun was rising again before we reached the bank of the river with our first loads of meat.

To the sportsman who hunts for trophies of the chase from a well-provisioned camp and at the correct season of the year, this killing of a cow moose in the middle of summer must no doubt seem a despicable performance. Yet I can assure him that, although a big pair of antlers are a more lasting triumph, and long afterwards may serve to dispel the doubts of his grandchildren as to the fact of his having been a remarkably fine fellow in his youth, there is no present satisfaction like that of bringing a load of meat, cow or bull, summer or winter, into a camp where provisions have been all too scarce for a season. Your men are really pleased that you have been successful in your hunt, and instead of the growl that with half-breeds and Indians usually follows the order to go and bring in the head, everybody is glad enough to rush off and bring in as big a load of meat as he can carry.

At the foot of the rapid, which we came to know as Slate Rapid, to distinguish it from others that we passed, we set up the lodge, and built stages for drying meat, as the weather was too warm and the flies too plentiful to keep fresh meat for any length of time. And then, for three days, we relapsed into the habits of the Indian, and held one of those meat orgies so dear to the heart of men who hunt their livelihood in the northern forests, and only to be really enjoyed after a lengthy period of hard times. During these three days it rained in torrents, and, in fact, for the last month there had been very little fine weather. I should imagine this heavy rainfall to be an exceptional occurrence, as the whole appearance of the country was typical of a dry climate. The water in the river reached its highest level on 25th June, and after that date fell quickly and continuously. When the rain once stopped, a spell of bright hot weather set in, which lasted till we neared the mouth of the Yukon, without any rain except an occasional thunderstorm. The gravel bars in the river were bright with flowers of many varieties; butterflies, especially the big black and yellow swallowtail, were in considerable numbers, and summer had fairly begun.

Below the rapid, the river continued its course to the south-west, with many windings and a good current of about four miles an hour. Islands soon began to show up in mid-stream, and the gravel bars must be of great size during low water, although now they were nearly wholly submerged. Cut banks of sand and stratified gravel, or sometimes black clay, were frequent, and the timber increased in size and was more freely interspersed with cottonwood as we dropped down stream. Now that we had abundance of meat on board, we often saw moose swimming the river, or standing up to their bellies in the water to keep clear of the flies, but we always left them unmolested, and they seemed to take little notice of the canoe unless we happened to pass to windward of them. It is a great pity we did not see all this game before we reached the main stream, as, if we had found means of supporting ourselves, I should certainly have waited a week or two for the water to go down, and then pushed on as far as possible towards the head of the river. But it was too late to turn back now, as a day's run down stream means a long distance when you have to fight your way back against the current.

A few miles below the rapid two large creeks come in from the north, but on the south side there is only one creek of any importance until the mouth of Campbell Creek, which enters at a distance, by rough reckoning, of 35 miles below the rapid, the main direction of the Pelly being now more westerly west. Campbell Creek was named by Dr. Dawson, who followed it down in 1887 when making the portage from Frances Lake; and close to its mouth is the site of the Pelly Banks Post. But we did not succeed in finding any trace of the old buildings.

We had now come to the end of the unexplored

PELLY RIVER AT THE JUNCTION WITH HOOLE RIVER.

part of the river, and the rest of our journey on the Pelly, a distance of over 300 miles, was made easy by consulting Dr. Dawson's account of the river and the excellent maps which he has published with this report.

A large stream, the Hoole River, so named by Campbell after his interpreter, joins the Pelly 33 miles below Campbell Creek. It is a wide shallow river, coming in from the southward and heading among the Pelly Mountains, which here run parallel to the river at a distance of 10 miles, and seem to be an open grassy range, surmounted by square rocky summits of great elevation. At the mouth of the Hoole River there is a rather formidable rapid on the Pelly, with a heavy sea during high water. There is an easy portage on the north side, but, by lightening the canoe, we ran through in safety, though not without shipping a good deal of water. This rapid should be run on the north side, with a sharp turn to the right just off the pitch of an overhanging bluff; and, by keeping just outside the eddy, the water will be found comparatively smooth. A good-sized boat might be allowed to follow the current, but for a small canoe the sea is dangerous on the left side of the channel.

Here the appearance of the country suddenly changes, especially on the north side of the river. Open grassy benches covered with groves of small poplar take the place of the denser forests, and, at

HE HAD GIVEN ME ENOUGH CHANCES.

a short distance back from the river, willow-covered swamps and little lakes are frequently met with. In these spots, on almost any evening, by climbing some small elevation, you can see a moose taking his evening feed, or, by watching the long grassy benches you may, towards sundown, see a couple of black spots shambling along the side hills, and know that you can probably get a shot at a bear if there is no meat in camp.

One evening, I saw a grizzly come out of the woods as I was smoking a pipe on a small hill overlooking the wild stream of Hoole Cañon, a few miles below the Hoole River, and, as he was so close, I thought I might as well try for some bear meat. But while I was stalking him, he had been travelling quickly towards me, and I was suddenly surprised to find him eating berries in a patch of wild-currant bushes within ten yards of me. I raised the rifle quickly but could not induce it to go off. Five times the cartridge snapped, and the bear went on with his currants, but when I worked the lever to throw up a fresh cartridge, he came to the conclusion that he had given me enough chances, and ran like a rabbit for a thick grove of poplars. When he was well among the trees the rifle roared off in grand style, and, of course, missed the bear. A fighting grizzly, such as are always encountered by the whisky-shop bear-hunters of the West, would have had a splendid opportunity of displaying his powers that evening at Hoole Cañon.

CHAPTER XII

DOWN THE PELLY AND YUKON RIVERS

Portage at Hoole Cañon—Varieties of mountain sheep—Ross River—Macmillan and Stewart Rivers—Difficulties of prospecting—Granite Cañon—Fort Selkirk—The Lewes River—First run of Salmon—Government officials and gamblers.

HOOLE CAÑON is by far the worst impediment to navigation in the whole course of the Pelly-Yukon from the Lakes to the Behring Sea. It is absolutely impassable for any kind of boat. I afterwards met a miner at Forty-Mile Creek, on the Yukon, who told me that a party of prospectors had once run through Hoole Cañon in safety, but I think he must have been testing my credulity, as I took a good look at the water while we were making the portage, and feel sure that any man who enters Hoole Cañon from above goes to his death. The current sets full on to the face of the bluffs in many places, there are several rocks in mid-stream, and besides a heavy sea, the whirlpools, as seen from above, look extremely dangerous. We found two or three small rapids just above the cañon, but these can be run easily, and the landing-place for the portage will be found immediately above a wall of white quartz on the left bank of the river, just where the stream bends sharply to the north-eastward. It is as well to have a man ashore along this quartz bluff, ready to catch a line, as during high water the current is swift, and a heavy swell makes it rather an awkward landing for any lightly-built boat. If this landing is once passed, nothing can keep you from going through the cañon on your voyage to destruction.

The portage is half a mile long, and passes over a lightly wooded hill of a hundred feet in height, with a sharp descent at the far end. The trail is well marked by a few of the old skids used by the Hudson's Bay Company's boatmen in dragging their boats across the portage, but at high water the canoe should be carried a couple of hundred yards lower down, as there is no convenient spot for loading up at the end of the trail. There are two or three ugly little rapids just below the cañon, when the river is in flood, but these can be run by a carefully handled canoe.

Ten miles down stream the Pelly is joined by a pretty little tributary named Ketza River, after one of Campbell's Indians. It comes down with a rapid current from the Pelly Mountains, which here approach the main river more nearly than at any

THE HEAD OF HOOLE CAÑON.

other point in its course. These mountains are probably inhabited by mountain sheep, as they look to be splendidly suited to that animal's tastes, and in an old Indian camp at the cañon I found two or three sheep's skulls, besides several scraps of skin. The horns were exactly like those of the big-horn of more southern latitudes, and the skin gave no signs of the gradation of colour known to exist between the true Ovis Montana and the Ovis Dallii of the northern mountains. But if my rifle had been in more serviceable condition, I should certainly have hunted the Pelly range, and tried to gather some information with regard to these sheep, as I cannot help thinking that too little attention has been paid to the widely different appearance presented by the mountain sheep in different localities as higher latitudes are gained, and it is very rarely that any authority on North American fauna makes mention of the big-horn, except as he appears in his better known haunts in Wyoming, Montana, or British Columbia.

It would take a man a long lifetime to follow up all the Indian stories he may hear in the North of a high mountain many weeks' travel from the nearest trading-post, whereon there exists a kind of a sheep which has only been seen by the narrator; yet a good deal of information might be obtained with regard to the distribution of the big-horn, and the variation in its appearance, if the men in charge of the outlying posts of the Hudson's Bay and Alaska Commercial Company were asked to collect a few of the skins from the Indians—who of course never bring unsaleable skins in without being specially told to do so—and to forward them, when they send out their yearly shipment of furs, to anybody who was interested in the subject.

Ten miles below the Ketza, Ross River joins the Pelly from the north. It is about the same size as the Pelly, and is, as far as we could see, a fine, navigable stream, heading towards the north-eastward, but its upper waters have never been explored. The same remark applies to all the large tributaries entering the Pelly-Yukon from the north-east, with the exception of the Porcupine, which joins the main stream at old Fort Yukon just below the Arctic Circle, and has been used for many years by the Hudson's Bay Company as a trading route from the Mackenzie to the Yukon.

The sources of the Ross, the Macmillan, and the Stewart Rivers—three really large streams, draining an immense tract of country on the western slope of the Rocky Mountains—remain quite unknown, although the lower part of the Stewart was for a few years the scene of a fairly prosperous mining camp. Of course, the prospecting and exploration of these streams is a matter beyond the capability of the miners, and cannot be carried out without a good deal of expense. The distances are so great, and the up-stream work so laborious during the few short months of summer, that it is a whole season's work to reach even the mouth of one of these rivers. The buying and transport of provisions for two summers and a winter would prove a heavy strain on the prospector's pocket, and the second season would be again occupied in travelling, with little time for working the bars. So that there is really little inducement for miners to undertake a long expedition of this kind, and probably many years will have passed before the long strip of country between the Porcupine and the Liard attracts much attention. The assumption is that it is worthless except for the mineral wealth it may contain, and there are still large tracts of land more accessible, and presumably more fit for settlement in various parts of Canada, that will occupy the Government surveyors for some time to come.

The tributaries entering from the southward are, of course, much smaller, as the strip of country lying between the Pelly and the Lewes is of comparatively small extent. They are all of the same character — shoal, rapid, and rocky, contrasting strongly with the deep, steady flow of the rivers that have their sources in the main range of the Rockies.

We prospected most of the streams, but never obtained any satisfactory result, although colours of gold may be found on nearly all the gravel bars.

The distance from the Ross to the Macmillan is given by Dr. Dawson as 173 miles, without any impediment to canoe navigation, although there are many small rapids. The worst of these is close to the mouth of the Glenlyon, which comes in from the south, midway between the two large streams, but it can be run without danger at any stage of water. In several places the river broadens out and is much broken up with islands separated by narrow, winding channels. Among these islands we were always sure of finding geese in great quantities. The young birds were well grown by this time and often gave us a good chase on the long gravel bars which were showing up as the water fell, but unless we could run them down in the open, they generally escaped in the thick growth of willows. Moose were still seen frequently, but as long as we could make a living with the wild-fowl we left them alone. Foxes are remarkably numerous all along the

Pelly, but, with the exception of lynx and a very few beaver, the other fur-bearing animals seem to be scarce.

In this stretch of river we often noticed rafts tied up to the banks, evidently used by the Indians for crossing the Pelly, but we did not fall in with any of the wandering bands. It is curious that they do not use canoes on such an easily navigable stream, but prefer to pack a load on their backs and make a straight course for their hunting-grounds, crossing and recrossing the main stream to cut off a detour, and only camping on its banks when they know that the salmon are running. Their fish-drying stages may be seen at every suitable spot, but it was as yet too early for the salmon to have covered the long distance from the sea.

The country still maintains its pleasant appearance—open, grassy benches lie close to the river, and small cottonwoods cover the rolling hills in the background. The immediate banks of the river are sandy, or gravelly buffs, with sometimes a long stretch of black, frozen earth. These places should be avoided when the ground is thawing out, as huge pieces of the bank are constantly falling into the water, and the overhanging trees of course come

SHOOTING A RAPID.

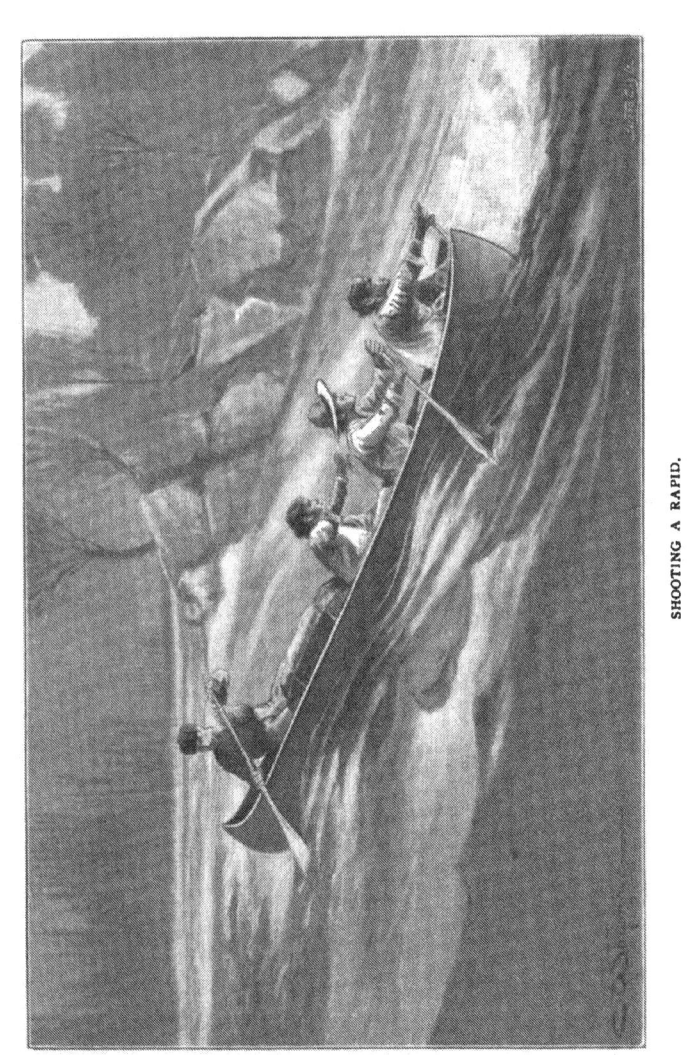

down at the same time. We camped for the night at the mouth of the Macmillan, which is very little smaller than the Pelly, and looks a most inviting stream for exploration. Miners have followed its course for a short distance by boat, but, not finding any paying bars, they returned without making an attempt to examine the upper waters. They reported no impediment to navigation as far as they went.

A few miles below the Macmillan we entered Granite Cañon, the last stretch of strong water on the Pelly. It is not a formidable cañon, and can be easily run by any kind of a boat or canoe. A shallow-draught steamer might probably be taken through with judicious warping at one or two of the points where the water is strongest, if there should ever be any necessity to take supplies above the cañon.

From this point to its mouth, the Pelly-Yukon is a placid stream, affording a good inland waterway through the interior of Alaska, and making it easy and fairly economical to open a mining industry throughout an immense territory which, but for the existence of this navigable river, would be one of the most inaccessible regions in the world.

Seventy-four miles below the Macmillan, on 8th July, we came to the confluence of the Lewes, and a couple of miles below landed at Fort Selkirk, an outlying trading-post situated on the west side of the main Yukon. Here we found ourselves in comparative luxury, and as some miners had just passed down stream from the head of the Lewes we heard all the latest news from the outside world. But there is always a feeling of regret on emerging from the woods into the semi-civilisation of a mining district, and in this case it was especially noticeable. With the exception of the small encampments of Indians on the Frances River and Lakes we had seen no human being since leaving the Lower Post on the Liard, and had been entirely self-reliant in finding our way through a long stretch of wilderness, but now we had reached the common highway to a mining camp, the most interesting country lay behind us, and the rest of our course lay down an easily navigated river, through a well-known country where we should miss the element of uncertainty as to what lay ahead, and should be able to buy provisions from the trading-posts instead of hunting them for ourselves. The men were of the same way of thinking, and as soon as the first glamour of the high living was over they came to the conclusion that paddling down the long stretches of the Yukon was too easy work, and everybody would have welcomed a rapid or even a portage as a change from the monotony of the long uneventful days that now ensued. Fort Selkirk stands in a convenient position for both the Indian fur trade and the constant summer trade of in-going and out-coming miners who have been tempted to try their luck in the far-off diggings of the great river of Alaska. Most of these miners leave the salt water at the head of Lynn Canal in May, and haul their summer supplies on sleighs across the high mountains by the Chilkoot Pass, aiming to arrive at the Lewes in time to build boats in readiness for the break-up of the ice. Several lakes lie in the course of this stream, and if the ice is still sound many of the miners continue hauling their sleighs till they reach the running water, as time is valuable in these northern latitudes, where the open season is all too short for a man who really means to work instead of being merely a hanger-on to a prosperous camp. After the ice has broken, the down-stream run of 600 miles to Forty-Mile Creek is easily made, as there are only two cañons where portages are necessary, but of course the return in the autumn is a different matter altogether, and involves much labour and frequent hardships. If a man is working a paying claim, and yet does not wish to pass an eight months' winter in inactivity, the question naturally arises as to how long he is to continue mining and leave himself time to get out of the country before he is caught by the running ice in the upper waters of the Lewes, or exposed to the terrific storms which are said to be frequent on the summit of the coast range during the autumn months.

The Lewes River was discovered by Campbell in 1842, during his exploration of the Pelly, and was named by him after one of the Hudson's Bay chief factors. A fort was established at the confluence of the Lewes and Pelly in 1848, and maintained for several years, but it was finally pillaged by the coast Indians from Chilkat and Chilkoot, who discovered that its existence interfered with their own trade with the tribes of the interior. No resistance was possible for the few inhabitants of the post, and they were ejected without bloodshed, the Indians taking off as many of the trading goods as they could carry, and escaping the attack of the local

Indians, who were friendly to the whites. No exploration of the Upper Lewes seems to have been made at this early date, but the existence of a pass to the salt water was well known to Campbell, and irregular communication seems to have been held by means of travelling Indians with the Hudson's Bay steamer trading on the Alaskan Coast. Sir John Richardson, in the narrative of his voyage down the Mackenzie in 1848, mentions having received Honolulu papers of late date, which had undoubtedly come by this route.

Nothing is now visible of the old fort except the pile of stones that until recently formed one of the chimneys, but its place has been taken by the less romantic buildings of a modern trading-post, around which a few Indian shanties are clustered. There is also a Protestant Mission just established, an outpost of the new Yukon Diocese founded by the Church Missionary Society, and presided over by Bishop Bompas, so well known for many years as the Bishop of Mackenzie River; but it is doubtful whether much success can attend the enterprise, as the Indians have been for some time exposed to the influence of the miners, which has always proved disastrous to the native tribes both morally and physically. Fort Selkirk is now supplied by one of the Alaska Commercial Company's stern-wheel steamers, which meets their deep-sea boat at St. Michael's Island, the nearest convenient landing to the mouth of the river, a very different state of affairs from the trading of Campbell's time, when a limited stock of the most necessary articles reached the old post by way of the Great Slave Lake and the Liard and Pelly, after a three years' journey from England.

Some attempt has been made at Fort Selkirk to raise a crop of potatoes and other hardy vegetables, but so far the result has not been satisfactory, owing to the late frosts in the spring, followed by the great heat and little moisture of the summer. Lower down the river, however, in the rainy districts, as the coast is neared, although in a more northerly latitude, some of the Catholic Missions show well-stocked garden patches, and at the mission school at Korykovski a large supply of potatoes is produced every year. From Fort Selkirk to Forty-Mile Creek, a distance of 230 miles, we took advantage of the perpetual daylight to travel at night, and slept while the sun was high.

The scenery from the river is not strikingly grand, a succession of irregular mountains lightly covered with spruce and poplar, alternating with dried-up grass, bounds the view in every direction, and one misses the high snow-capped peaks that attract attention during a journey along the Liard or Pelly.

On the night of 9th July we passed a large encampment of Indians, and learned from them that the first of the salmon had arrived. An all-important event is this annual run of salmon to the numerous natives who dwell along the banks of the Yukon and its tributaries. Three weeks before the fish reach Fort Selkirk, the various tribes of Esquimaux at the mouth of the river are laying in their provisions for the winter. Thousands of traps, to say nothing of the countless numbers of scoop-nets, have to be passed by the salmon along the course of the river before they reach the Pelly Lakes, where the moose-hunters are lying in wait for them late in the autumn. Far up the Tanana, among the Alaska Alps, and in the foot-hills of the Rockies at the head of the Porcupine more traps and more nets are in readiness to work destruction on the salmon. On the lesser streams that head among the dreary swamps of the tundra encircling the Arctic and the Behring Seas, the same scenes are enacted year by year—men, women, and children engaged in killing and curing the fish that are the staple food of the vast native population of Northern Alaska. And the supply never seems to have failed. There are no stories of years of starvation, which are only too common among the meat-eaters to the eastward of the Rockies, and as yet there are no canneries to thin out the fish on the Yukon, as has happened on most of the salmon rivers of the Pacific. Doubtless before long there will be suggestions to establish canneries, but unless the strictest regulations as to their management are enforced, there will be hard times for some of the upper river Indians. Along the Columbia and Fraser, neither of which streams were so thickly peopled as the Yukon, other means of making a livelihood were afforded to the Indians as the farming land was settled up, but there seems no likelihood of the same thing occurring on this northern river, as the country is worthless from an agricultural point of view, and if the salmon disappear, the Indian must go with them.

At the encampment below Fort Selkirk we saw

the finest birch bark canoes—shapely little crafts, longer and narrower than the bark canoes on the eastern rivers, as they seem to be built especially for poling up stream, and for this work are more easily handled than the broader canoes of the Crees and Chippeweyans, though less serviceable in rough water. The poling is always done by a man sitting amidships, with a short pole in each hand, and by keeping close in shore, a long distance can be made in a day, even against a rapid current. From these little canoes the salmon are caught by drifting down stream with the scoop-net held in readiness to strike as soon as the sharp eye of the fisherman detects the first slight wave of the advancing fish, which is soon afterwards in the hands of the women, undergoing preparations for the drying stage.

On the same night we passed the mouth of White River, a wild stream that would be considered a large river anywhere except in this land of great waterways. It heads away to the westward among the high glaciers of the Mount St. Elias range, and the reason of its name is at once obvious. Such a rush of thick, milky wash is discharged into the Yukon that the whole volume of water in the main stream is discoloured from the junction of the White River to the sea, and below this point it is always preferable to take drinking-water from any of the small incoming creeks, although the contribution from the White River seems to possess no unhealthy properties, and is freely used by the Indians along its course.

A few miles below White River the Stewart enters from the opposite side. Mining operations have been carried on with good results for some years past on this stream, but at present little gold dust is coming out, and most of the miners have left the camp. An old trading-post at the junction of the rivers was unoccupied at the time of our visit.

After another short run we came to another new establishment on an island opposite the mouth of Sixty-Mile Creek, and were told that if we wanted gold dust, we had better buy a supply of provisions here and start at once up Sixty-Mile Creek to the new diggings, which gave sure promise of proving immensely rich. The trader was incredulous when I told him that we were not mining, and were only running down the Yukon as the shortest way out of the country. He finally came to the conclusion that we were either Government officials or gamblers — apparently the only professions left open to the traveller on the Yukon who is neither miner, trader, nor missionary.

While lying on the bank at Sixty-Mile Creek during the heat of the day we felt a very distinct shock of earthquake, and it seems that in the summer months these shocks are of rather frequent occurrence though never of great severity.

These names of Sixty-Mile and Forty-Mile Creeks are at first somewhat misleading, as one would imagine that the two places lay within 20 miles of each other, but the distances are taken according to the miners' calculation from the intermediate point of Fort Reliance—once the headquarters of the early traders. Further complication has arisen since these stretches of water were measured and found to be considerably at variance with the estimated distances from which the creeks were named.

CHAPTER XIII

FORTY-MILE CREEK TO FORT YUKON

Forty-mile Creek—Miners' law—Boundary line between Alaska and British Columbia—Arrival of the *Arctic*—Coal Creek—Ovis Dallii—The Yukon Flats—Route from Athabasca to Behring Sea.

ON 11th July we reached Forty-Mile Creek, and, shooting out of the dirty flood of the Yukon into the clear water of the creek, pitched our lodge on its bank in a clump of willows a mile above the cluster of log cabins which forms the capital of this northern mining district. The peculiar build of our canoe and our own ragged appearance created great interest in the little town, and we had many questions to answer as to the mining prospects of the country we had passed through. The lodge was full of visitors all day, and I soon made the acquaintance of all the leading citizens of the creek. The total summer population of the district was estimated in 1893 at a little under

400 miners, of whom perhaps 150 would remain to winter at Forty-Mile Creek, and the rest had come in to see what chance there was of making a stake, and intended to go back to the coast in September. Of course, at the time of our arrival, work was in full swing, and, as the diggings lie at a long distance up the creek, there were very few miners in the town. The latest excitement was the new strike on Miller Creek, where three or four claims were really paying well, but there is no excuse for the grossly exaggerated reports that have lately been circulated in regard to the richness of the Yukon placers. During the last two summers, 1894-95, men have been crossing the Chilkoot Pass in hundreds, expending the little capital they had in the costly transport of supplies to Forty-Mile Creek. The result is sure to be disappointment in nine cases out of ten, and the unfortunates will have to depend on the charity of the storekeepers for provisions enough to take them to the coast. It seems hard to understand who is to be benefited by these reports of great wealth to be found in hardly accessible countries, but it is certainly a fact that, the greater the distance and the obstacles to be overcome on the

way, the greater the rush will be for the land of promise. Mr. MacQuestion, the trader at Forty-Mile Creek, who, by the way, is exceedingly good to anybody stranded in the country, does his best to issue true reports as to the state of the mining camps; and the men of several years' standing on the diggings are also very careful not to over-estimate the yield of gold dust, but still once again it has happened that a few paying diggings on Miller Creek have caused an influx of a rather undesirable class. At present, the tone of the camp is distinctly good, the real workers are the old timers from the Californian and British Columbian mines—men who have seen the difference between camps that were run subject to law and order as administered by the late Sir Matthew Begbie in the days of the Cariboo diggings, and those where the whisky bottle and six-shooter held sway. Up to the time of my visit, there had never been a killing on Forty-Mile Creek, although the law was not represented by gold commissioner or police, but was left entirely to the decision of the miners' meeting—an excellent court as long as the better class of men are in the majority, but a dangerous power in the hands of the vile specimens of humanity who sooner or later get the whip hand in most of the mining camps. Whisky had at times found its way into the camp, and the frightful concoction known as "Hootchinoo," distilled from molasses, has caused some trouble. But so far the sale of intoxicating liquor to Indians had been almost entirely prevented. The miners' meeting has pronounced that whisky is good and shall be allowed for the whites, but if any man sells it to the Indians after he has been warned he shall be punished; and the miner's idea of punishment is strictly Draconic. It is senseless to keep a man in gaol and pay another man to look after him. It is far better to warn him once and hang him for the next offence. Really, a very sound law this, in such an isolated district, where the Indians are in great numbers and are known to become hostile to the whites when under the influence of liquor, to make the man who is really responsible for any bloodshed that may occur suffer the full penalty in anticipation of the trouble that his degrading traffic is sooner or later sure to bring about.

In the winter of 1887-88, Mr. W. Ogilvie,

Dominion Land Surveyor, was sent by the Canadian Government to establish the boundary line between the United States possessions in Alaska and the North-West Territories of Canada, in the neighbourhood of Forty-Mile Creek, with the view of ascertaining on which side of the line the Yukon diggings were situated. His observations, corroborated by those of the American surveyors sent to the north for the same purpose, gave the result that the boundary line crosses Forty-Mile Creek at a distance of about 8 miles from its mouth. The little town is therefore put in an anomalous position, being distinctly an American town, getting its supplies from San Francisco in American bottoms, with an American post-office selling American stamps, and the whole town situated on Canadian soil. The mines on Forty-Mile Creek are well within Alaska, but the Stewart River camps are Canadian, as is also, of course, the site of the trading-post at Fort Selkirk. In 1893 there was no Canadian or American customs officer on the whole length of the Yukon, and unless trade should assume greater proportions, there was little need to alter this state of affairs, which seemed admirably suited to all whom it concerned. The

Canadian moderation in this respect contrasts favourably with the action of a United States officer at the old Hudson's Bay Post of Fort Yukon, at the mouth of the Porcupine, in 1869, who reported to his government as follows: "On the 9th of August, at 12 M. I notified the representative of the Hudson's Bay Company that the station is in the territory of the United States; that the introduction of trading goods, or any trade by foreigners with the natives, is illegal and must cease; and that the Hudson's Bay Company must vacate the buildings as soon as practicable. I then took possession of the buildings, and raised the flag of the United States over the fort."

The account of the miners as to the output of gold dust on Forty-Mile Creek was discouraging, and all the men who had spent several years in the district agreed in saying that there never had been any rich camps on the Yukon. No big fortunes had been made, but if a man was willing to work, and was contented with a moderate reward for his labour, fair wages could usually be made during the short season that was available for mining. Most of the profits are, of course, used up in buying provisions for the winter, but with the advantage of continual water carriage from San Francisco, the price of provisions is not so high as might be expected, and the expenses of coming in from the coast in the spring and returning in the fall are nearly as great as the cost of wintering in the interior, without taking into account the loss of working time. But it is no country for the lazy man or for the gamblers and tough characters that usually attend mining camps, and such people until lately were in no demand at Forty-Mile.

But now this primitive method of self-rule is to be done away with. During the past summer news has come out from Forty-Mile Creek of a shooting scrape brought about by a dispute over a poker hand, and resulting in the death of two miners. It seems that the camp can no longer be trusted to govern itself. A detachment of North-West mounted police, though dismounted to suit the exigencies of the country, has been sent up to the Yukon to keep the peace. A customs-house officer went up at the same time to levy a tax on all American goods brought in to Canadian territory. The chief result of this move will unfortunately be that the wretched miner will have to pay a still greater price for his provisions, while the revenue of the Dominion can hardly be increased sufficiently to pay for the expense of keeping up officials on the spot.

On the main stream of the Yukon, a little above the mouth of the creek, stand the church and other buildings of Bishop Bompas' Mission, and a mile or so below are the store buildings of a new company which has lately started an opposition to the Alaska Commercial Company's trade on the Yukon.

A little competition will be welcome enough to the miners, but if the output of gold dust does not rapidly increase in value the trade will be hardly worth competing for.

During our stay at Forty-Mile, the river steamer *Arctic* arrived, sixteen days out from St. Michaels, but she brought me no letters of credit, which I had been expecting to meet me here. MacQuestion, however, although he knew nothing at all about me, kindly supplied me with provisions enough to take us down the river, and I expected to meet my letters at some point farther down stream. By the way, it is most necessary in this part of Alaska to be properly provided with either money or some sort of credentials, as the old hospitality and readiness to accept a man's word for his respectability has been forced out of existence by the conduct of former travellers; and the Alaska Commercial Company have been so often imposed upon, that orders have been reluctantly given to the men in charge of the small posts along the Yukon to demand immediate payment for all supplies furnished to strangers, and if no money is forthcoming, to give them only provisions enough to make sure they shall not starve before they reach the next post. The direct cause of this edict was, I believe, the conduct of a large party of miners who had really done rather well in the diggings. They drifted down the Yukon to St. Michaels, where they declared they were destitute, and were fed for a week or two and finally given free passage by the company's steamer to San Francisco. On landing, they paid in $5000 worth of gold dust to the Mint, and were loud in their boasts as to the astuteness they had displayed in getting ahead of the Alaska Company. This sort of thing has made rather hard going for impecunious people on the 1500 miles run from Forty-Mile Creek to the sea. From the captain of the *Arctic* I tried to get information about the chances of getting away from St. Michaels in the autumn, but he could tell me nothing definitely. The company's steamer might call there late in September, or she might have got through her work by the first of the month. The United States Revenue ship *Bear* usually came into St. Michaels about the beginning of September, and would take passengers to Ounalaska, if there was no chance of their being able to catch any other steamer at St. Michaels; but of course she had no fixed dates of sailing. I learned, however, that there was an alternative route, by leaving the Yukon two or three hundred miles from its mouth and crossing to the Kuskokvim River, which lies to the southward. From the mouth of the Kuskokvim we could coast along the sea to the head of Bristol Bay, and if there was no direct communication from there to Ounalaska, we might still be able to cross the portage across the great Alaska peninsula and reach the sea again at Katmai or Cook's Inlet.

Before leaving Forty-Mile I secured good homes for all the sleigh-dogs. They had been of the greatest service of course while the snow lasted, but they had proved a great nuisance in the canoe, besides being a heavy strain on the provisions. Our pace of travelling down stream was too fast for the dogs to run along the densely wooded banks, so we had to take them on board, where they were always in the way, and increased the danger of running a rapid by jumping on top of the cargo and adding to our instability whenever orders were given in a loud voice, mindful of the long winter days spent in harness when a shout was too often accompanied by a crack of the whip.

On 18th July, late in the evening, we tore ourselves away from the luxury of the mining camp, and drifting down a few miles, pitched our lodge at the mouth of Coal Creek, an insignificant stream coming in from the eastward, with the intention of hunting a high range of mountains which were said to be frequented by mountain sheep. I had seen some of the skins at Forty-Mile, and, as they were very white, with the tips of the hair looking as if they had been singed by fire, I presume these sheep are referable to the variety Ovis Dallii. On the tops of the mountains I found plenty of tracks where the sheep had evidently been travelling in the spring, but their summer feeding-grounds must lie to the northward, in an extremely rough, irregular range which still carried patches of snow on the summits. I should have made a further expedition into this distant range, but Alick, who accompanied me as provision-bearer, utterly disappeared in the thick brush at the foot of the first hill, and I saw no more of him until my return to camp after two days, during which time I made an easy living by shooting marmots and ptarmigan, which are in great abundance on the grassy summits. From a very elevated position I had a good view of the surrounding country, which seems to consist of irregular rolling hills near the river valley, with high open plateaux in the distance. On some of these plateaux the cariboo wander in their thousands, and, as they frequently cross the river, form an invaluable winter food supply to the miners. Their passages are uncertain, however, and although sometimes they cross Forty-Mile close to the mining camp, and are then slaughtered in great numbers, there have been several winters when the want of fresh meat was severely felt, and scurvy played havoc among the bacon eaters.

A few miles below Coal Creek I killed a moose, and a couple of days were spent in drying the meat. Moose or black bear supplied our wants all the way down the Yukon, although the bears had flavoured their flesh very strongly with the rotten salmon they find in such quantities on the river bars. As long as these animals stick to the berry patches, their meat is really good, but when the salmon begin to run, they all come down to the streams, and the fishy taste is noticeable in their flesh almost immediately. We saw no grizzly along the main stream, although we were told many and terrible stories of their deeds of violence.

And now the navigation became most monotonous. There is something fascinating of course in the idea of running a couple of thousand miles down a big river, but the charm is lost as soon as the rapids are passed, and the element of danger is taken out of the day's work. We could make 80 to 100 miles a day with ease in twelve hours' actual paddling, with an early start and putting ashore to eat every four hours. But there was too much sitting down in a cramped position, and we missed the excitement that is always to be found in canoeing on a smaller stream; there were no sharp corners to round with the chance of running into something below the bend, but long smooth reaches stretching away to the horizon fringed by a dense growth of willows, and all so exactly alike that one loses his admiration for this immense river in the weariness which its monotony produces.

After leaving Coal Creek we had a long steady

run of 300 miles to Fort Yukon, situated on the peninsula between the Porcupine and the Yukon, at the lower end of a vast maze of islands and winding channels that must formerly have been a lake in the course of the river.

The breadth of the Yukon at this point has never yet been determined, but is variously estimated at from 10 to 70 miles, according to the miners' fancy. As a matter of fact nobody has ever travelled much along the west side of the river here, as the best channels are on the Porcupine side, and no doubt, too, there is a great difference in the breadth of the Yukon in high water and low at this point. The current runs strongly through the narrow channels, which keep splitting up and rejoining so rapidly that it is very hard to pick out a practicable way through the labyrinth, as the smaller channels are choked with snags and fallen timber, besides being sometimes very shallow at the lower end. In the autumn, when the water is low, the steamer has great difficulty in passing up this part of the river, as the sand is continually shifting, and a bar may have been formed in what was deep water on the occasion of the previous voyage. Our little canoe frequently grounded in some of the smaller channels, but we made no attempt to keep the main channel, and took any opening in the bank that fancy dictated, never with any worse mishap than having to wade a few hundred yards. The islands are covered with cottonwood and willow, or more rarely with a scattered growth of spruce, and the whole country near the river is so level that no mountains are in sight for a distance of 200 miles along the course of the river. This district is locally known as the Yukon Flats, and is one of the best places for wildfowl on the whole of the upper river. Geese were very plentiful, as were also mallards, widgeon, and teal, besides large numbers of gulls, terns, and divers. We did no fishing, as we could always get salmon from any of the Indian camps that we passed every day, and I noticed that the women were catching some fine whitefish in short rawhide nets, set in the small eddies, although they seemed to be thought of little value while the salmon were running.

In the early forties, while Campbell was making his discoveries on the Liard and Pelly, the Hudson's Bay Company, with characteristic energy, was sending exploration parties across the Rockies of the

WILD-FOWL ON THE YUKON FLATS.

Lower Mackenzie to make an examination of the Porcupine, with the result that trading posts were established along its course as far as its junction with an immense river flowing to the westward. It was, however, left for Campbell to prove that this was the Pelly-Yukon of his own explorations, and this he satisfactorily accomplished by running down from Fort Selkirk to Fort Yukon, and returning to the Mackenzie by way of the Porcupine. It at once became obvious that this new route was preferable to the difficult navigation of the Liard, and to-day the traveller can leave the Hudson's Bay Company's landing on the Athabasca, and travel continuously down stream, with the exception of the short ascent of Peel River and the Rocky Mountain portage to Fort St. Michaels, on the shore of the Behring Sea—a distance of 4000 miles —with scarcely any more trouble, and perhaps less risk than is involved in a transcontinental railway journey.

Since the evacuation of Fort Yukon, there has been no trading carried on there till this last summer, when a storekeeper has put up new buildings a short distance from the site of the old fort, to open up a trade with the Indians of the Porcupine.

On the latter stream the Hudson's Bay Company have just shut up their establishments, as the Yukon posts could easily undersell them, and the Indians think nothing of taking their furs 300 miles farther to reach the best market.

And here we came to the most northerly point of our journey, for the Yukon, after just crossing the Arctic Circle at the mouth of the Porcupine, trends away in a south-westerly direction, finally reaching the sea in latitude 62° N.

CHAPTER XIV

THE KUSKOKVIM RIVER

Tanana River—Bones of the mastodon—Murder of Archbishop Seghers—
Ikogmut—Kuskokvim River—A game country.

A COUPLE of hundred miles brought us to the Tanana, the largest of all the Yukon tributaries, having its sources in the unknown fastnesses of the Alaskan Alps. The Tanana is much used as a winter route by travellers from the Lower Yukon to Forty-Mile Creek, as it cuts off the big bend of the main stream, and there is only a short portage from its upper waters to the mining camp. Besides this, the number of native villages where salmon can be procured every night for the dogs save the carriage of extra weight—always a most important consideration to the dog driver.

At the American Church Mission of Niklukyet, standing on the north side of the river below the confluence, we met a number of the Tanana Indians, who had come down to trade, the best looking natives that we saw among the fish eaters, and quite in keeping with their little birch-bark canoes, which I think show a prettier model than any other bark canoes that I have seen throughout Canada or Alaska. These Indians told us of an easy way to the coast that might be found by poling for two days up the Tanana, and making a day's travel with many small portages up and down little streams and through several lakes, till a creek tributary to the Kuskokvim is reached. The latter stream is a clear stretch of water passing through a good game country, and without dangerous rapids, to the Behring Sea. I should much like to have taken this portage, but I thought my letters might reach me at any point on the main stream, and without them our finances would not bear the strain of hiring guides. It is hopeless for a stranger to try any of these short cuts for himself, as the traveller possessed of local knowledge will vary his course every time he passes through the strange maze of slowly-moving water-courses that drain the level country adjacent to the Yukon and the Kuskokvim.

Below the Tanana we saw no moose, and after

another day's run no tracks were to be seen on any of the bars. The Tanana itself is said by the Indians to be a good moose country throughout, and there are rumours of great abundance of these animals in the district lying between that river and the head of Cook's Inlet. The isolated mountains lying in the tundra, which now begin to show up, are also said to be frequented by moose, but the valley of the Lower Yukon does not seem suited to their habits.

Along this part of the river the Indians frequently brought us mastodon teeth and huge bones, which they were anxious to trade for tobacco. At one place they showed us a long stretch of high muddy bluffs, where these bones are frequently exposed as the strong current washes down the banks; but we found nothing of interest, although we took a great deal of risk in peering about under the crumbling masses of muddy shale which keeps continually falling into the river. It is probable that the Indians had carefully picked up anything of value, as a good mastodon tooth will usually fetch a plug of tobacco from the passing miner.

We put ashore early one morning at a little trading post to have a talk with a Russian Finn whom we had heard of, a man who had seen forty years of service in Alaska, and under happier circumstances was, no doubt, able to give us reliable information about the portage to the Kuskokvim, and the journey along the sea coast that lay before us. He came out to welcome us kindly enough, but I saw he was not quite right when he began to shake hands with us from the top of a bank 30 feet high, and finally slid down to the canoe in a sitting posture, with his hand still stretched out in greeting. He had been drinking "hootchinoo" before the sun was up, with disastrous results, and judging from the amount of fiery stuff still left there was little chance of his sobering up that day. He was most hospitable, but could only talk of the glories of San Francisco, where he had spent the last winter, and refused to say a word about local matters that might have been of some interest. I thought it prudent to escape before the "hootchinoo" proved too much for my crew, and take the chance of finding the way for ourselves, so we pushed out into the current and left the old fellow waving the bottle on the bank.

At Nulato, 200 miles from Niklukyet, the climate seems to change as the influence of the sea makes itself felt. At the time of our arrival the rainclouds were driving up the river in front of the west wind, and the rest of our journey along the Yukon was made against a head wind and heavy sea, with nearly continual rain—a great change from the long spell of hot, dry weather that had lasted with hardly a break from the Slate Rapids on the Pelly to Nulato.

On the bank of the Yukon, some 20 miles above Nulato, stands the cross erected to commemorate the murder of Archbishop Seghers, who was here killed by his servant in 1886, while on a visit of inspection to the Roman Catholic Mission stations along the river—one of the most cowardly, purposeless crimes ever committed. A mild rebuke had been administered by the Archbishop overnight for negligence in some small matter, and that, according to the Indian who was travelling with them at the time, was the only reason to account for the murder. Early in the morning the servant, a white man, got up and lit the fire, shouted "Breakfast ready," and shot his master as he raised himself up in his blanket.

At Nulato the old mining talk was again heard. Some new diggings had been discovered several hundred miles up the Keokuk, and promised to be as rich as all other new diggings. A stern-wheel steamer was running right up to the mines, and several men were making preparations to spend the winter at the new camp; but some who had returned gave less hopeful accounts, and complained that the gold dust was not to be found in the expected quantity.

The Keokuk joins the Yukon from the northward, a short distance above Nulato, and forming a big northerly bend heads back towards the neighbourhood of Fort Yukon. The Indians from the head of the Keokuk were the perpetrators of the celebrated massacre of the natives of Nulato, and their name is still in bad odour among the lower river tribes, but of late years no disturbance has taken place.

At this point there was a noticeable mixture of the Esquimau type of face among the salmon fishers, and a few long, slender, walrus-skin canoes were to be seen hauled up with the birch-barks in most of the camps. There was a difference, too, in the native dress, and here we first saw the parka, a long, sack-like garment worn by men and women alike in common use—usually made from the skins of cariboo or ground hogs, but the wealthier members of the Nulato tribes wore the skins of the Siberian reindeer, which are obtained from the Esquimaux, and fetch a big price among the Indians of the interior. Although Nulato is, by the course of the river, many hundred miles distant from the salt water, its inhabitants are brought into close contact with the coast tribes by means of a short winter road that reaches the sea at Norton Sound.

With the arrival of the steamer came another disappointment; there were no letters again, and it became evident that we must once more rely on our own skill as hunters and fishermen to keep the pot boiling, and limit our purchases to the barest necessities. Smith had a little gold dust that he had brought from Cassiar, which afterwards proved of the greatest service, as there was absolutely no credit to be had. All the trading-posts were in charge of Russian half-breeds, who could speak no English, and lost all interest in us when they discovered that we had no money with which to pay for what we wanted. The most serious inconvenience we felt was from the scarcity of blankets and clothing, as the weather was nearly always wet, and would, of course, be cold along the sea coast as the autumn approached. There was nothing to be done, however, except to continue our journey in the old rags that we had brought from the Liard. I afterwards heard that all this trouble had been caused by the carelessness of the postmaster at Forty-Mile Creek, as my letters of credit from the Alaska Commercial Company's office in San Francisco had been lying there at the time of our arrival.

Another run of nearly 200 miles took us to the little village of Anvik, where a Protestant Mission has been established. It stands, like all the other settlements, on the north or sunny side of the Yukon, and is cut in half by the Anvik River coming in from the tundra lying to the northward, and available as a short route to St. Michael's. For any traveller who has a light canoe, and wishes to avoid the rough piece of coast work from the mouth of the river to the ocean steamer's landing on St. Michael's Island, lying some distance to the north of the delta, this Anvik River ensures a speedy and easy journey, as the long detours of the main river are avoided, and the portages through chains of lakes are said to be short and not of frequent occurrence.

Sixty miles below Anvik is Korejovski, the headquarters of the Roman Catholic missionaries, where the well-filled school buildings give evidence that good work is being done among the rising generation. The comparatively extensive farming operations give a more cheerful appearance to the place than is presented by any of the unkempt trading-posts that we had seen above, and the mission grounds are carefully fenced off from the filth of the native village, which seems usually accepted as a necessity. The children are kept neat and clean, in strong contrast to their friends and relations, but the tendency to fall back into the habits of long ages is hard to eradicate suddenly, and no doubt some time must elapse before cleanliness becomes tolerated for its own sake instead of merely as an irksome condition on which the good living at the mission school may be enjoyed.

Hay-making was going on busily in the intervals between the rainstorms; the cattle looked wonderfully homelike after our long sojourn among the moose and bear. The potato crop was looking well, and would form an important item in the winter's supply for such a large establishment, though the children only really thrive on the ever-reliable salmon, and become quickly disgusted with a continuance of the white people's diet.

After leaving Korejovski, we ran down to the Greek Church Mission at Ikogmut, a distance of about 70 miles, and camped just below the village in a heavy storm of wind and rain. Here Father Belkoff has been in charge of the mission for many years, and is probably one of the best living authorities on the early history of the Russian traders on the Yukon. He gave me the only reliable information that I had as yet received with regard to the portage to the Kuskokvim, and told me that the chief of the Upper Kuskokvim Indians was at present at Ikogmut, and would be leaving for home in a day or two. This decided the question as to routes, and, finding the men only too glad to leave the beaten track and get away from the monotonous windings of the Yukon, even at the risk of not being able to get passage to San Francisco till spring, I interviewed the chief of the Kuskokvims with the satisfactory result that he agreed to act as pilot across the portage. Father Orloff, the assistant missionary at Ikogmut, interested me greatly with his description of the upper waters of the Kuskokvim, where he had wandered in the course of a winter's journey. From his account of the game in the high mountains toward the head-waters of the river, it must be one of the most attractive countries still left untouched by the sportsman-explorer. He mentioned the same old rumour of another kind of mountain sheep differing totally from the bighorn and the mountain goat, which is well known to the Kuskokvim Indians, but he could say nothing definite about it as he had never seen it himself. Certainly the northern parts of the St. Elias and contiguous ranges are as likely a spot as anywhere on the American continent to find an animal unknown to science, for there is a very large and difficult tract of country from the head of Cook's Inlet to the big bend of the Yukon that has never been traversed.

On the 15th August we left Ikogmut in company with the chief and his family, who were travelling with a long, slim bidarka or skin canoe, and a small birch-bark. A heavy sea prevented our crossing the Yukon till evening, when we entered the mouth of a small creek with little current, winding between low banks covered with a thick growth of willows. Here we said good-bye to the river whose water had carried us so well on our long down-stream run from the Pelley Lakes, and I heard regrets expressed that we were forcing our way through mud and wind and rain towards civilisation, instead of seeing the leaves turn yellow in the dry uplands by those distant lakes where the moose and cariboo were fattening for other hunters.

For a whole day we paddled up this winding creek, which split up so frequently that nobody without local knowledge could possibly keep the right course, and at sundown camped fairly on the edge of the tundra, carrying the canoe and part of the cargo over the first portage to a small lake. A gloomy, desolate strip of country is this marshy tundra, with its countless lakes and sluggish streams, especially as we saw it this night in drenching rain, which only seemed to pause a few moments to give the mosquitoes a fair chance to annoy us. But there was still enough willow scrub for firewood, and even a few spruce trees were scattered about over the long stretches of morass, rendering the landscape far less wearisome than in other parts of the tundra, where there is absolutely nothing to break the dull gray level.

Two days were occupied in poling through shallow lakes, where the rushes and water-lilies almost prevented the passage of the canoes; in making portages, sometimes by carrying, and sometimes by dragging over the soft mud, and in following the windings of the creeks up and down stream, round sharp corners, where collisions with the bank were unavoidable. The long bidarka was the worst offender in this respect, but the banks were soft and no damage was done. Wildfowl were in such numbers as are to be seen only in these northern breeding-grounds, and our companions showed great dexterity in knocking down rising mallard or teal or swimming musk-rats at short range with a three-pronged spear. Often the women insisted upon being put ashore where the yellow berries of the muskeg were thickest, when bladders of unsavory seal oil and a few handfuls of sugar that had been brought from the traders' store at Ikogmut were produced, to mix with the fruit.

As the weather now became unusually fine, we took things easily, killing geese or ducks as we wanted them, and it was late on the third evening after leaving the mission that we dragged down a long slough with scarcely enough water to float us, and found ourselves at the Kuskokvim. Here our pilots left us, as their way lay up stream, and after a trifling present of tobacco, and many signs of mutual satisfaction—for the chief's half-dozen words of Russian conveyed no meaning to me, although he had used them many times over in conversations on the portages or round the camp-fires—we shot out into the swift current and soon left our friends far behind.

The Kuskokvim is by no means a small river, but, of course, does not approach the Yukon in size. It has more current than is found in the Lower Yukon, which runs a course of several hundred miles in winding through the low-lying country adjacent to the sea. The Kuskokvim takes a more direct course, and its banks are drier and more pleasant to camp on than the swampy shores of the Yukon. The salmon run was nearly over, and few fish were being taken in the traps that were staked off at the head of nearly every gravel bar. Native villages were frequently met with, and the total population of the Kuskokvim must mount up to a very respectable number, although I believe many of the fishermen we met were not residents, but had come from various parts of the coast to catch their winter supply of salmon. The villages are built in the typical Innuit style, a collection of half-underground barra-boras or earth-houses, each flanked by one or two square wooden rooms raised on high stilts above the risk of floods, as a place of safety for the stores of dried fish and other treasures of the simple-minded native. Birch-bark canoes are entirely replaced by a great variety of models in walrus skin, from the great family boat in which the women, children, and household gods travel from place to place, down to the little kayak, in which the Innuit hunter spends most of his existence during the summer months.

An uneventful run of 100 miles brought us to a trading-post built on the north bank of the Kuskokvim, just where the river begins to broaden out into the curious funnel-shaped expansion by which it finds its way to the sea. Here, too, stands a Moravian Mission, offering yet another choice of creeds to the savage, who surely must be rather bewildered by so many conflicting theories as to how his future welfare may best be ensured. The missionary was extremely good to us in smoothing our way with the trader—a Russian half-breed speaking no English, and very loath to part with any of his provisions for the scanty supply of gold dust that represented our whole capital. We eventually secured a little flour and a fair stock of leaf-tobacco to trade with the Innuits for fish or any other necessaries we might be in want of.

Everybody advised us strongly against the rashness of proceeding to sea in our little canoe, and doubtless the advice was well meant, but there seemed to be no way out of the difficulty, as nobody offered to give us a more suitable boat or to advance us a winter's supply of provisions if we remained where we were. The missionary gave us the best description he could of our route, and told us that we could avoid some of the rough water by making use of the small rivers and lakes, with a few portages, if we could pick up guides on the way who would pilot us to Nushagak.

CHAPTER XV

ON SALT WATER

Coast navigation—The Innuits, their food, habits, and dress—Moses and Aaron—Good News Bay—A scene of desolation—Kayaks—Cape Newenham.

On 23rd August, in rags and poverty, we started down the tidal water in an open canoe to navigate 300 miles of coast-line utterly unknown to us, and exposed to the fury of one of the stormiest seas in the world. At various distances along this coast were native villages, and from their inhabitants we were to obtain provisions if we ran short, and to gather information as to what lay ahead, although we could not speak a word of their language. At the very outset we found that we had undertaken a task which would involve a good deal of time and some risk. Only 50 miles down we were obliged to lie quiet on the marshy bank for a day and a half till the westerly gale moderated, and the sea went down enough to allow our canoe to make her way in safety. During this time we were surprised to see a large schooner running up the river in midstream, but the sea was too heavy for us to go out and speak her. No vessels had been expected at the trading-post, and I hardly liked to turn back on the chance of getting a passage to the southward by the stranger, so we continued down stream as soon as the weather was good enough for travelling. The Kuskokvim had now increased to such a width that the northern shore was invisible, but, as the country is a dead level, without any tall trees on either side, the distance across is probably not more than 7 or 8 miles.

Villages were still frequent on the south bank, and continued at longer intervals along the sea coast till we reached Nushagak. The Innuits, as the natives of the sea coast are called from the mouth of the Yukon to the head of Bristol Bay, are probably the most numerous of all the Esquimaux tribes. A simple, kindly race, hospitable to the passing stranger, but indescribably filthy in appearance and habit. They make an easy living off the salmon which run in thousands up every little stream of the tundra, the hair seals which breed among the outlying rocks, and the walrus which are still fairly abundant in parts of the Behring Sea. The fur seals do not come in on this coast at all, and are too far off at sea for the Innuits to reap any benefit from the decision of the Behring Sea Arbitration Congress, which forbids the use of firearms for the killing of seals, in order to give the native a chance of employment.

So far these people have pretty well escaped the contamination of the white men, as their settlements lie out of the track of whalers bound for the Arctic Sea, and the whisky sellers do not like to venture too near to the dangerous coast.

It is a pity that the American Government is so fully occupied in watching the movements of a few foreign sealers that it cannot keep an eye on the movements of its own whalers; perhaps it is because the fur seal is a distinct source of revenue and the wretched Innuit is not.

Of late years the San Francisco whalers have been pushing on farther and farther round the shore of the Arctic Sea towards the Mackenzie River, and the damage done among the natives is already noticeable, but nothing is done to prevent it increasing. It is true that a very flagrant case a few years ago caused some comment in the newspapers, but it seemed to be nobody's business to make an official inquiry into the case.

Late one autumn a whaler on her return voyage brought up in front of a populous village on an island in the northern part of the Behring Sea. A lively trade ensued with the natives, who were anxious to make their bargains quickly and go in pursuit of the walrus which were now passing, and which every year provided the winter's food supply. But in addition to the legitimate articles of trade, a couple of kegs of strong rum were put ashore, and the schooner sailed away for San Francisco with all the wealth of the village in her hold.

By the time the natives had finished the rum and got over its effects the walrus had all passed, there was no supply of food put up for the winter, and ice was beginning to drift in the sea. The result was inevitable. The next whaler that called at the island was able to take home an interesting collection of bones and skulls of the Esquimau type to an ethnological institution, but there was no man, woman, or child left alive on the rum-stricken island to tell the story of starvation and death.

When we approached any of the Innuit villages the women always turned out and sat on the roofs of their turf-houses to get a better view of the strange boat, while the men came down to show us the best landing, and help us run the canoe up quickly beyond the reach of the surf. They always lent us poles for setting up the lodge, and gave us firewood when there was no drift timber near. They have to make long expeditions up the small rivers for poles, as they require a good many for setting their fish traps in deep water, and none of a suitable length grow anywhere near the coast. The inside of their barraboras smelt too much of rancid seal oil and general filth to be comfortable quarters for a white man at this time of year, although they would make a snug enough shelter from the savage winds that sweep this dreary coast in winter.

The natives were liberal, too, with their salmon, and would always give us a good supply for a leaf of most villainous tobacco. But they could never understand our preference for fresh fish to those in various stages of decomposition. Some of their freshly smoked salmon are really very good, but most of them are spoilt to a white man's taste by being tied up tight in bales before they are properly dried, and allowed to turn sour. On one occasion I objected to some fish which an old man brought into the lodge as not being fresh enough, and made signs to that effect, chiefly with the aid of my nose. The old man went away and brought some more which were far worse. On these being rejected he beckoned me to come with him, and leading me to a swampy spot at the back of his barrabora pointed out what I took to be a newly made grave. I made signs of interrogation and deep sympathy, whereupon he scraped away the loose earth with a fish spear and lifted a board which covered the top of the pit. I fully expected to see the body of a dearly beloved relative, and experienced nearly as great a shock when I found the pit was filled to the brim with a seething mass of rotten salmon. The old fellow's next signs I fully understood; they were to the effect that if I wanted something really good I must give him more than the usual amount of tobacco leaves, and I began to realise that he had misunderstood my sign language and thought I was objecting to his fish because they were too fresh.

The salmon pit I afterwards found was a common

institution at every village, its contents being usually reserved for winter use.

The dress of the Innuits is simplicity itself, the parka being the only really necessary garment for either sex. On this part of the coast the ground-hog supplies all the clothing, and, after the salmon run is over, every Innuit woman makes a summer's expedition to the nearest mountain range to snare ground-hogs for the yearly wants of her family, while her lord and master is spearing hair seals, or perhaps hunting walrus under the high cliffs of Cape Newenham. A few of the women make their parkas by stitching together loon skins, which are pretty enough while new, but soon drop their feathers and are not nearly as serviceable as the ground-hog skins. A pair of shapeless sealskin boots reaching half-way up the leg completes the regulation outdoor costume, although members of both sexes wear a pair of white linen trousers as a tribute of respect to the advance of civilisation for a week or two after a visit to the nearest trading-post. But once inside the barrabora even the parka is discarded, and men and women squat on the filthy mud floor as naked as their fathers and mothers did long ages before the trousered missionary appeared on the shore of the Behring Sea.

At the mouth of the Kuskokvim immense mudbanks, which are dry at half-ebb, make the navigation difficult for large vessels. A canoe or shallow draught boat should come out a little before high water, as there is then water enough to float her close to the shore, and the first of the strong ebb will take her to the southward across the banks before she grounds with the falling tide. We did just the wrong thing — as so often happens to strangers—and left the mouth of the river about three hours after high water. A seal hunter was coming in in his kayak, and gesticulated to us wildly to come ashore, but we took it for granted that he only wanted us to land to give him a leaf of tobacco —which is a common trick of the Innuit. Our mistake soon became evident, as we found we had to keep round a bank which ran off several miles to sea, and with a strong ebb meeting an onshore wind there seemed a good chance of getting into trouble. A landing through the surf meant probably the loss of everything, and a long struggle through soft mud to reach the firm shore.

The canoe behaved very well, and by occasional

baling we rounded the outside point in safety, and had both wind and tide in our favour till a bend in the channel brought us close to the mainland just as darkness came on. Here we landed and carried the canoe and cargo to a pile of stranded logs which we made our home for the next four days, while the Behring Sea was swept by such a storm that many a bigger vessel than ours would have been glad of a snug harbour.

In the morning we found that we had put ashore close to the warehouse used for storing the trading goods for the Kuskokvim district, which are here lightered ashore from the Alaska Commercial Company's steamers and afterwards taken up the river in skin-boats. As it was evident that we could not move till the wind moderated, and rain was pouring down continually, we were forced to set up the lodge with poles borrowed from a native burying-ground, where each man's grave was adorned with a row of spears and paddles, and in one case a wonderful specimen of an ancient flint-lock gun. Poles are planted at the head of every grave to mark its position when the snow lies deep, as the natives have a dislike to walking over their dead. Here we struck up a lasting friendship with a couple of Innuits, who had also taken refuge from the bad weather, and, by means of the various signs which suggested themselves, made a bargain with them to act as pilots to Nushagak. It afterwards transpired that they had never been there, but apart from this they turned out to be good fellows enough, thoroughly trustworthy, ready to lend a hand in any emergency, and always cheery, except in heavy weather, when they became often needlessly alarmed for the safety of our canoe, which would ship water in a sea that broke harmlessly on the skin decks of their own kayaks. They answered readily to the names of Moses and Aaron, bestowed on them by the half-breeds, who took a great fancy to them at once. Aaron had a shrivelled leg, which made him quite useless ashore, but in his kayak he was as good a man as anybody else. Some former traveller has conferred a great benefit on his followers by establishing the half-dollar as the standard of trade between whites and natives along this part of the coast, so that when an Innuit scratches a round mark in his palm with the forefinger of the other hand, it means half a dollar, instead of the dollar always represented in this manner in other parts of America. But for small trading, tobacco is universally used, as men and women are intensely fond of it and can never afford to buy any quantity from the traders. They seldom use a pipe, but soak the tobacco in seal oil, roll it up in a ball, and find great satisfaction in chewing it.

When a gale of wind is blowing the rainclouds on shore, the meeting-place of the tundra with the water of Behring Sea presents a picture of muddy desolation that could hardly be surpassed in any part of the world. Land and water are so strangely intermixed at the various stages of the tide that it is difficult to choose a spot for the camp that will remain above the sea level, or to tell which pool will yield fresh water for the kettle. The floodtide runs with a strong current far up the incoming rivers, which find their way across the tundra till the banks are overflowed and salt-water lakes appear where an hour ago there was nothing but an extra depth of soft mud to show that the land had recently been submerged. There is always an uneasy feeling, too, that there may be a big roller forming somewhere out at sea, a couple of feet higher than its neighbours, which will presently break upon the beach and wash everything before it to the foot of the isolated range of mountains standing far in on the tundra. And yet, directly the sun comes out and the wind moderates, it will be found that even this country has a charm of its own, in its suggestion of limitless extent, in the quiet colours of its grasses and flowers, in the changing moods of the sea, and especially in the great abundance of bird life that frequents the breeding-grounds of the coast in the early autumn.

On a fine evening, as you sit behind some great drift log that the Kuskokvim has borne hundreds of miles from the interior of Alaska, waiting for the evening flight of the geese which are to provide your day's rations for the morrow, and listen to the notes of the wild-fowl and plover out on the tundra, the beauties of nature seem to become more distinctly visible than during the rush of travel, when your attention is occupied with pole or paddle; and the attraction of the lonely desert at such a time will linger in your memory for many a day after the attendant storms and hardships are forgotten.

When we left the warehouse, a spell of better weather set in, and we were able to coast along the level shore without any more delay till we reached Good News Bay. Here the land rises, and gravelly beaches take the place of the muddy shores that characterise the estuary of the river. A pleasant enough shore to cruise by, with deep water close in, and usually plenty of driftwood to camp with, although there is absolutely no growing timber except the dwarf willow bushes. Whenever we had a fair wind we lashed the kayaks alongside, and, hoisting all available canvas, ran gaily as long as the water was smooth. In a heavy swell, the kayaks ploughed up such a high bow-wave that the water broke over our combings, and our companions had to be cast adrift, invariably falling a long way astern. In rough weather they had, of course, far the best of the fun, as the kayak can ship no water. The small round hatch in which the paddler sits is tied round with the lower part of a thin fish-skin coat, so as to be perfectly watertight. The coat is also tied closely round the neck and sleeves to keep water from entering by those means, and a round wooden hat renders everything secure. With his row of spears and a spare paddle lying on deck in a neat little rack ready to his hand, the Innuit will go to sea as long as he can force his little craft against the breeze.

At Good News Bay the mountains come down to the sea and are continued for a long way to the southward, till they terminate in the headland known as Cape Newenham. This appeared to be an ugly piece of coast for an open canoe, and I was rather pleased to find our pilots heading for the end of the bay, where a large village stands at the mouth of a river, whose course we were now to follow. For two days we pushed up this river, poling, towing, and wading in water that was already beginning to feel cold, through a dry rolling country with mountains of some elevation, till it became merely a deep little ditch, in some places too narrow for the canoe. When we could follow it no longer we began to abuse Moses for bringing us the wrong way, but he was quite equal to the occasion, and taking his kayak on his shoulders stalked off towards a grassy ridge that lay right ahead, making signs for us to do the same. About a mile away we found a little lake, but we had to cross the portage twice to bring everything over. Aaron of course was not much use here, but in spite of being crippled he always managed to carry over a light load. I took pity on him the first time and carried his kayak over for him, but never offered to do so again. The only way to carry one of these canoes is to put your head right inside the hatch and let her rest bottom up on your shoulders; but there is such a frightful stench of seal oil and rotten fish inside every kayak that was ever built, that one experience of a portage a mile in length is quite sufficient.

We made altogether five portages in passing through a chain of lakes, and finally dropped on to another little ditch draining towards the south-west. During this part of our journey wood was very scarce; in fact we had once or twice some difficulty in getting fire enough to boil a kettle. A big camp fire at night was quite out of the question, and we began to feel the want of blankets and better clothing, as there was always a sharp frost on clear nights, and the early mornings were wretchedly cold. The stream we now had to follow was merely a repetition of the last, but with the advantage of the fair current the navigation was much easier, and early on the third day after leaving salt water we reached a comparatively large river entering the Behring Sea, well to the eastward of Cape Newenham. At the junction of the streams we met a party of Innuits, who were bound for a cariboo hunt in a range of mountains already in sight to the northward.

Some little difficulty here arose about provisions, as we had grown careless of the future, and our pilots could usually spear salmon enough for present use. But just now they were at fault, and no wildfowl were to be found up these little rivers, so we had to apply to the strangers, who produced a rawhide net which they stretched across a small slough, with the pleasing result that thirty clean run sea-trout with an average weight of three pounds were brought ashore in five minutes, and an unexpected dinner was provided for all hands.

At the mouth of the river—which we reached at nightfall—there is another village, where we had no difficulty in trading tobacco for a supply of salmon sufficient to last us for several days. The existence of this fresh-water route had been a splendid thing for us, as during the three days that we had been travelling along the rivers a strong wind was blowing on the coast, and we should probably have been lying on the beach all the time unable to travel. Cape Newenham, a long projecting headland with a strong tide race is one of the roughest places on the Behring Sea, and there is said to be a long continuous stretch of high cliffs on which no landing can be made. If we had not come across our faithful

Moses and Aaron we could only have blundered on along the coast and trusted to luck in getting round safely, as it would be impossible for a stranger to follow the inland route by himself even if he knew of its existence.

Below the village is a large estuary, and from its lower end a narrow rocky channel leads through the surf into the open sea. This must be a dangerous spot for any kind of boat with a strong onshore wind, as we found some trouble in dodging the broken water when we crossed the bar in a dead calm, with an ebb tide meeting the least perceptible ground-swell. In the offing lie the high cliffs of Hagemeister's Island, a noted place for bear according to our guides, but time was valuable and the width of the intervening channel would have caused unnecessary risk to our frail vessel. On this same evening we were caught in a breeze, and being unable to keep the sea, were forced to run ashore through rather heavy breakers, which nearly caused a total wreck, and though the little kayaks came ashore without shipping a drop of water, they seemed to be in some danger of rolling over on the crest of a breaking wave. We did our best to land the cargo dry, but the sea was too much for us and nearly everything in the canoe was soaked. The poor Kodak camera, which up till now had been very lucky in keeping out of trouble, had to swim for its life, and all the photographs of the sea coast and its inhabitants were utterly ruined. In the morning a recurrence of the disaster was only avoided by wading out the canoe through surf up to our waists and climbing in one at a time when we got outside the breakers, a bad beginning to a long, cold day's journey. About 10 miles away in a straight line lay the point of Togiak Bay, which we had to round, but the wind was too strong to try the crossing, and even in skirting the land we found the sea quite heavy enough. At the head of the bay a large stream, the Togiak, comes in from the eastward, and at its mouth the ebb tide meeting a heavy swell made a confused broken sea on the shoal ground. Here we again shipped a good deal of water and had to bale out several times; but once across the mouth of the river there was a little shelter close to the land, and without further trouble we arrived at the wretched little hut which does duty for a trading-post, built close to the extremity of the point. A dreary, inhospitable place it seemed as we saw it, in wind and rain. Not a soul was to be found, as the trader was away, and although we could see an abundance of flour and other good things through the window of the store, there was no chance of getting at them except by force. By peering through a crack in the boards of the dwelling house we could catch a glimpse of a neat little pair of shoes, standing side by side on the floor, with very high heels in the middle of the soles, such as can be seen in great numbers pattering along Kearny Street on any fine afternoon. So, perhaps, the trader of Togiak leads a less dreary life than the natural surroundings of his habitation might suggest. We were not sufficiently hard up for anything to feel justified in helping ourselves, so we pitched our lodge and ate salmon and ptarmigan contentedly, while we waited for the strong south-west wind and heavy sea to moderate enough to enable us to leave the shelter of the bay. The camp-fire was supplied by driftwood, but there was still a total absence of standing timber, and the willow bushes seemed even more stunted here than in other parts of the tundra.

Ptarmigan were very plentiful and were beginning to band up into big packs, as is always their habit when autumn approaches. Geese were often seen in large numbers, but were not easily approached except on the muddy flats at the mouths of the rivers. Of the sea birds, the most conspicuous on this part of the coast were the cormorants, gulls, guillemots, puffins, auks, divers, scoters, and eider ducks. The only small animals we noticed were the red and Arctic fox, the mink, the musk-rat, and a small variety of the ground-hog or siffleur. None of the larger animals seem to come out to the sea coast. The only tracks we saw were those of an occasional bear on the sand-bars of some of the small rivers along which we travelled.

CHAPTER XVI

VOYAGE TO OUNALASKA

A gale of wind—Karlukuk Bay—Inland navigation again—Wood River—The schooner, her skipper and crew of many nations—Ounalaska—Homeward bound in the 'Frisco steamer.

THE wind freshened up into a gale with continual rain, and two days were lost at Togiak on account of bad weather. On the third day, although it was a bright calm morning when we started, we were sharply reminded that our canoe was not the right sort of vessel in which to attempt a coasting voyage on the Behring Sea. The shore here changes its appearance, and instead of the low sandy or gravelly beaches on which a landing can always be made with safety to life in case of necessity, long stretches of rocky bluffs begin to appear, precluding all hope for the occupants of any boat not seaworthy enough to keep an offing. As we were passing one of these bluffs, a sudden squall from the westward ruffled up the long ground-swell into a dangerous sea, and for some time it was doubtful whether we could keep the canoe sufficiently clear of water to round the next point in safety. To turn back and run with the sea seemed to offer a worse chance than pushing on, as the distance to run was much greater, and if the squall continued it was only a question of a few minutes till one of the short steep waves would break on board and render the canoe unmanageable, even if there was not weight enough in the cargo to make her sink at once. The kayaks stayed by us, and the Innuits gave us much advice that was no doubt well meant but utterly unintelligible. They were evidently greatly alarmed for our safety, and could have done nothing to help us in case of disaster. There was one little bight just under the pitch of the head where it might have been possible for an active man to climb the cliff if he were lucky enough to escape damage in the surf, and I had serious thoughts of trying it, although of course it meant total destruction of canoe and cargo, but a few more minutes' struggle, with some desperate plunges into the head seas, took us round the point in safety, and to everybody's relief a successful landing was made on a sheltered gravelly beach. We were only just in time, as the wind freshened up to the force of a whole gale, which blew with unabated violence for two days and nights, accompanied by heavy rainstorms. The canoe, propped up on her side, gave us a little shelter, but there was no driftwood to be found, and time hung heavily during the enforced delay. There was still a long ugly piece of coast ahead of us, but when the weather once moderated it continued fine until we had rounded the headland forming the west entrance to Karlukuk Bay, when the most perilous part of our journey was safely over. We paddled our best on this occasion, as everybody was anxious to avoid any recurrence of our experience after leaving Togiak.

At the head of Karlukuk Bay is another village, where our guides held a long interview with the inhabitants as to the best way of reaching Nushagak. Moses and Aaron had come to the end of their local knowledge, but still kept up their interest in us, and would not hear of our employing another pilot. They insisted too on acting as interpreters between the strangers and ourselves, and took great pride in showing their countrymen how well they could talk to a white man. It turned out that another stretch of inland navigation was available, a smooth-water route by which Cape Constantine—a promontory projecting far out into Bristol Bay—might be altogether avoided.

Starting from the village at low water, we carried the flood tide up the innumerable windings of a river entering the head of the bay. At the end of the tidal water the land rises quickly, and of course a strong current was met with at once. Shortly above this point two or three small swampy lakes lie in the course of the stream, and here the salmon were rotting in thousands, some dead and some making their last struggle, unable to ascend the stream higher, and apparently unwilling to turn their heads down stream to the salt water. Several portages from lake to lake occupied a good deal of time, but by noon on the second day out from Karlukuk we had crossed the last height of land and entered a sheet of water 8 miles in length, lying south-west and north-east, drained by a stream flowing towards the Bay of Nushagak. Spruce timber now began to show up frequently (the first we had seen since leaving the Kuskokvim), and increased in size as we ran down stream. A few miles down is a second lake about 4 miles in length, a very pretty stretch of water well wooded on all sides, and plentifully supplied with fish. At an Innuit camp the drying-stages were loaded with salmon of a much better quality than usual, besides a large stock of trout and whitefish. An old man, with a little Russian blood in his veins, and two good-looking daughters, keeps a small trading post at the north end of the lake, where he is looked upon with great respect as the representative of the powerful Alaska Commercial Company. His whole stock consists of a few pounds of tea and tobacco, but he evidently makes the most of these commodities, judging by the pile of furs that was stacked up in one corner of his underground house where he entertained us at a salmon feast.

The furs traded by the Innuits on this part of the coast are not of much value, being chiefly musk-rat skins and red foxes of poor quality. The beaver skins are very good, but these animals are not numerous, and the hunter has a long journey to make into the interior before he can expect to make a successful hunt.

On leaving the lake, the river, which is locally known as Wood River, is at first a succession of small rocky rapids, but the navigation is perfectly easy. Fifteen miles below the lake tidal water is reached, and from this point to the bay the course of the stream is exasperatingly crooked, while the flood rushes up with such force that it is more profitable to camp and wait for high water than to waste labour by paddling against the tide.

At last we reached the open sea and secured a local guide from a village at the mouth of the river, as the weather was foggy, and our own pilots had no knowledge of what lay ahead. After a little trouble with the broken water on the bar, we made our last camp on the gravelly beach of the bay, and the following morning reached Nushagak in good time. As we paddled up to the trading post, a schooner came beating down the river which here enters Nushagak Bay, and we at once recognised the vessel that had passed us on the Kuskokvim nearly a month ago. She was evidently bound for sea, but luckily stranded on a sand-bar, and we were able to communicate with her before the tide rose sufficiently to float her off. I had no time to examine the settlement, but it is doubtless a place of some importance, as there are several canneries on the river, and during the fishing season arrivals and departures of vessels connected with the salmon trade are common events. But by this time (18th September) the canneries were all closed and the summer's catch was well on its way to San Francisco. It was by the merest chance that we caught the schooner, and if we had reached the post a few hours later, we should have had several hundred miles farther to paddle, with some open sea work, besides the long fresh-water route by which the Alaskan Peninsula may be crossed to Katmai. At Katmai we should probably have been no better off than at Nushagak, as communication with the south would certainly have been closed long before we could have reached that point. Our experience in coasting along the Behring Sea had shown us that as long as we were travelling on the salt water, delays, if nothing worse, would be of frequent occurrence. Of the twenty-five days that had been spent on the passage from Kuskokvim Mission to Nushagak, when half the journey lay through fresh water, no less than nine whole days had been wasted in waiting for wind and sea to moderate. As the winter approached, the storms would most likely increase in duration and severity, so that there was every possibility of our being caught by the snow before we reached Katmai. The schooner bound for Ounalaska was too good a chance to miss, so I at once interviewed the captain, with the view of obtaining a passage by his vessel. I found him very full of a wonderful reformation in his own character, which had just been brought about by the missionary at Nushagak. "I left 'Frisco in May," he told me before I had been on board five minutes, "a roaring, godless sinner, the same as I always was, but that's all changed now, and I am a new man." That his conversion was real there can be no doubt, as he confined his roaring to the singing of Methodist hymns all the way to Ounalaska, and only showed symptoms of godlessness in moments of sudden excitement. The missionary deserves full credit for this, and it is a pity he could not have kept the worthy skipper long enough to teach him the rudiments of charity and goodwill towards his fellow-men. It proved no easy matter to get a passage in the reformed man's schooner, as he had no intention of helping strangers out of the country merely as an act of charity, and we were most unlikely-looking objects from whom to obtain the exorbitant number of dollars which he demanded for our passage to Ounalaska.

The company's agent at Nushagak knew nothing about me, and as far as he was concerned we had done remarkably well in being able to pay off our Innuit guides at his store, leaving a very few grains of gold dust in our treasury. A compromise with the captain was at length struck. He held an examination of all our personal effects, and came to the conclusion that they were of sufficient value to cover the price of our passage to Ounalaska. On arrival there, if none of the Alaska Commercial Company's officials would guarantee my respectability, the captain was to take over my possessions and put us ashore. If, however, I should prove to be more solvent than he expected at present, I was to have the option of continuing the voyage to San Francisco in the schooner, at another exorbitant rate, in case the last steamer had already left for the south.

We paddled alongside in a heavy rainstorm, and hoisted the canoe and cargo on board. Moses and Aaron came off in their kayaks to see the last of us, and received more treasures of dirty clothes and worn out knives, axes, and kettles than they had ever seen before in their lives. Our long journey was practically over, although there were still 400 miles to be covered before we reached Ounalaska. But the method of travelling was changed; a strong wind which might have obliged us to camp a day or two before, would now be welcome enough, and in this rainy sea the cabin afforded many comforts that were noticeably wanting on the beach. The schooner was one of those mysterious crafts that cruise in lonely waters without any ostensible business—a flat-bottomed, centre-board scow, utterly unfit to work off a leeshore or to make a passage to windward in a seaway. I did not like to inquire too closely into the purposes of her voyage, and of course could only guess at the skipper's reasons for spending a long summer among the natives of the northern seaboard. The whole visible return cargo consisted of fifteen live reindeer and a couple of Arctic foxes. The crew were a strange mixture of human beings. The mate had begun life behind a counter in Glasgow, but was now Americanised into the worst type of blow-hard anti-Briton. He had committed some breach of discipline, which must have been fairly slack in such a ship, and had been put in irons for a week or two, till the cook refused to carry him his meals any longer. When I met him at

Nushagak he was under orders from the captain to consider himself in irons for the rest of the voyage. This seemed to suit him exactly, as he kept no watch at night and played cribbage with the half-breeds all day.

There were two deck hands, one a fair-haired Norseman of 6 ft. 4 in., who would have looked more in place hurling spears from a viking ship than steering a rotten flat-bottomed American schooner, and a good little Scotchman who had served a rough apprenticeship in an east-coast herring boat. The cook was a fat German who talked a good deal about beer, and was always ready to leave his pots and pans to shout advice as to the navigation of the ship. Yet this schooner had made a long summer's cruise, from San Francisco to the Siberian shore of the Behring Sea, always escaping damage from the numerous shoals on which she grounded, and eventually reaching San Francisco safely, late in the autumn.

The voyage to Ounalaska was made in seven days, without any unusual incident: for two days we drifted in a fog off Cape Constantine, and for the same length of time beat against a head wind and sea, without gaining any distance. Then the wind came fair out of Bristol Bay, and the schooner wallowed along under the high volcanoes of the Alaskan Peninsula, and the outlying chain of the Aleutian Islands, with the sails wing and wing, the pumps working at intervals, and the captain roaring for "Beulahland" in the cabin, instead of looking after his navigation. When we had run our distance there was some difficulty in finding the entrance to Ounalaska harbour, as the gray clouds hung over the land, and only the foot of the long line of cliff was visible. A day was lost in standing off and on waiting for clearer weather to enter the bay. We saw a good many fur-seals on this day, and could have made a successful hunt, but our captain had enough on his conscience already, and would not take any extra risk of losing his ship by confiscation for having seal-skins aboard, when schooners engaged in the business were being seized on sight by the ever-watchful American cruisers.

At the office of the Alaska Commercial Company I was able to pay off the skipper, as my letters of credit had arrived a couple of months before. A steamer was expected down from St. Michael's in a week's time, and would sail at once for San

Francisco, so we deserted the schooner, as there was no object in continuing our rather uncomfortable voyage.

Ounalaska has for many years been a place of some importance, as besides being the northern headquarters of the Alaska Commercial Company, it lies directly in the track of whalers bound for Point Barron and the Arctic Sea. Since the beginning of the Behring Sea dispute, Ounalaska has become the rendezvous for British and American ships engaged in patrol work to watch the movements of the sealing schooners, and carry out the terms of arbitration. Recently a new company has started up in opposition to the Alaska Commercial Company, with large buildings at Dutch Harbour, within a couple of miles of Ounalaska; and coal depots for supplying the gun-boats have been established. A fortnightly mail service to Sitka brings the settlement a little nearer to civilisation during the summer months, but in winter communication is altogether cut off.

The United States Revenue cruiser *Bear* was lying in Dutch Harbour when we arrived, and her officers were always ready for duck-shooting and fishing expeditions, so that time passed pleasantly enough till the middle of October, when the steamer from the north came in. After a long stormy passage on the North Pacific, with a call at Kodiak, we finally landed at Nanaimo, the coal mining town on Vancouver Island, at the end of the month, and my crew immediately took the train for their homes in Manitoba. They had behaved wonderfully well during the whole trip, and proved reliable from start to finish, ready in emergency, and very little inclined to grumble. This is all the more creditable as they had never travelled on salt water before, and knew nothing of tides and storms and breaking seas; but they took everything as it came without remark, and waited for an explanation of these strange things till the day's travel was over and a fire of driftwood lit up the surf that for ever plunges on the shingle beaches of the Behring Sea.

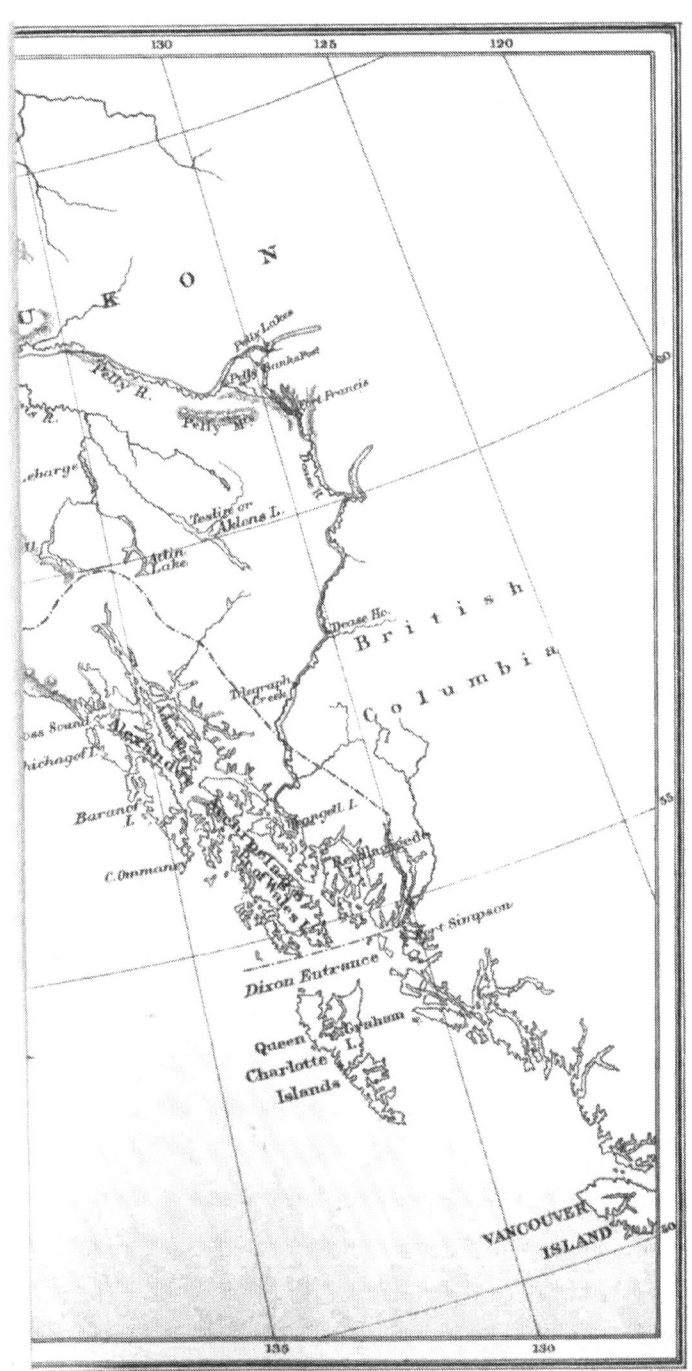

F.S.Weller, 42, Denmark Hill.

APPENDIX

I

A LIST OF GEOLOGICAL SPECIMENS COLLECTED BY MR. WARBURTON PIKE NEAR THE HEAD-WATERS OF THE PELLY RIVER.

Professor George M. Dawson, Director of the Geological Survey of Canada, has been good enough to arrange the collection.

1. Four specimens from low foot hills forming west side of valley of Yus-ez-uh. 4th May.
    Gray fine-grained cherty conglomerate, with greenish quartz, apparently forming veins.
2. Two specimens from bluff 10 miles up Yus-ez-uh. 6th May.
    Black slaty argillite.
3. Two specimens drift from rocky bar at outlet of Macpherson Lake. 8th May.
    Association of quartz and calcite, the former running through the latter in narrow ribs. Evidently from a vein.
4. Four specimen rocks from bluff forming cañon on stream flowing towards the foot of Macpherson Lake from west, about 3 miles up. 10th May.
    Gray-green schist and fine-grained gray limestone.

5. Four specimen rocks from same spot. 10th May.
    Gray fine-grained limestone and glossy gray schist.
6. One specimen from exposure on small hill on south side same creek, 5 miles up and half a mile back from creek. 11th May.
    Ferruginous and calcareous sandstone.
7. Two specimens from bluff on south side same creek, 8 miles on the portage. 12th May.
    Gray coarse-grained quartzite.
8. Three specimens from mountain across same creek, on portage 10 miles in, forming west spur Too-Tsho range. 12th May.
    Gray granite, containing both hornblende and mica, also pieces of small white quartz veins.
9. Two specimens drift from south shore of main Pelly Lake. 6th May.
    These are worn pebbles. One of dolomite and quartz, interpenetrating. The other a fine-grained red and greenish rock, probably an argillite.
10. Two specimens from exposure on side of low mountain on south side Pelly River, 2 miles above lake. 17th May.
    Fine-grained highly ferruginous sandstone, apparently associated with dark argillite. Also a rounded pebble of fine-grained greenish felspathic rock.
11. Three specimens from track, east end of Pelly Lake. 23rd May.
    Fragments of rusty quartz and of quartz impregnated with a little green ferriferous dolomite.
12. One specimen from same spot.
    Fine-grained blue-gray limestone, with interbedded gray calcareous argillite. A pebble irregularly weathered.
13. Two specimens from exposure on conical hill, half a mile from west end of second lake. 25th May.

Green-gray quartzite-like rock. Fine grained, probably somewhat felspathic.

14. One specimen from cañon, 18 miles above Pelly Lake, on south side river. 27th May.

Pale greenish-gray quartzite, with schist of same colour.

15. Two specimens from north side, same cañon. 27th May.

Light gray cryptocrystalline quartz carrying pyrite. Found on assay to contain neither gold nor silver.

16. One specimen from bar 15 miles above Pelly Lake. 27th May.

A purplish fine-grained bedded rock, of which some layers are highly calcareous and some siliceous. The weathering out of the calcareous layers has given the fragment a form somewhat resembling that of a bone.

17. Two specimens from bluff 15 miles above Pelly. Boulders of similar rock scattered over the hills. 27th May.

Purplish, slaty argillite.

18. One specimen from hill, west end second Pelly Lake. 28th May.

Gray glossy schist, apparently felspathic.

19. Two specimens from hill north side of same. 28th May.

Finely bedded blackish argillite schist, also a fine-grained felspathic rock.

20. Two specimens from bluff on small lake to south of same. 29th May.

Gray quartzite, ferruginous and slightly calcareous. White quartz veins.

21. Two specimens from cañon above third Pelly Lake. 6th June.

Green-gray glossy schist.

22. One specimen from bluff near source of Pelly. 7th June.

Gray glossy schist.

23. Eight specimens from mountain side at source of Pelly. 8th June.
> Fine quartzose conglomerate and slightly schistose quartzites, composed of granitic debris. Small quartz veins. Also gray calcareous schist and gray limestone associated with schist.

24. Three specimens from heap showing through swamp near source of Pelly. 9th June.
> Iron ochre, highly calcareous, porous structure, perhaps a gossan.

25. Two specimens from Pelly above third lake.
> Dark blue-gray fine grained limestone, also a piece of ferruginous quartzite with small quartz veins cutting it.

26. Four specimens from bluff, north side of main lake, one mile from outlet. 17th June.
> Fine-grained gray calc-schist.

27, 28, 29, 30, 31. Collected from numerous bluffs along cañon of Pelly, below the chain of lakes, and after junction with large streams coming in from northward during the day's run of 30 miles. 22nd June.
> 27. Black slaty argillite.
> 28. White cleavable calcite, with minute fissures holding compact limonite (var. glaskopf).
> 29. Black slaty argillite, slightly calcareous, small quartz veins.
> 30. Hard ferruginous sandstone. Gray where unweathered.
> 31. Green impure (sandy) limestone, sometimes dolomite. Veinlets of calcite and dolomite.

32. Seven specimens from rapids 35 miles below Pelly Lakes. Slate in greatest proportion. 23rd June.
> Gray and blackish schist, very slightly calcareous, holding numerous small cubial pyrites crystals.

Also a fine conglomerate chiefly composed of gray chert fragments.

33. Four specimens from bluff 3 miles below rapid. 26th June.

Fine-grained greenstone (Diabase?) also a fine-grained association of quartz and dolomite, evidently from a vein.

34. Two specimens from large bluff south side of Pelly. 28th June.

White quartz with iron stains.

35. Two specimens from dry cañon entering Pelly from northward. 28th June.

An association of white sub-translucent to opaque quartz, with bright green chromiferous serpentine.

The specimens collected by Mr. Warburton Pike, about the head-waters of the Pelly River, include no fossils of any description, nor are they accompanied by any notes on the strike or dip of the beds from which they were obtained. The locality of each is, however, marked upon a rough sketch map of his route, supplied by Mr. Pike.

Lithologically, they are somewhat varied, and are evidently derived from a region of considerable disturbance in which no one rock is continuously represented over any considerable area. Generally speaking, they do not differ much from the series of rocks met with and described in my report [1] on the Yukon district, as occurring on adjacent parts of the Frances River and Lake and the Pelly River. They appear to show the continuation of a similar association of stratified formations throughout the new country traversed by Mr. Pike in 1892.

Unfortunately, the geological examination of all this part of the Yukon district has, so far, been insufficient to establish the normal succession of formations in it, and the clue which might

---

[1] *Geological Survey of Canada, Annual Report.* New Series, vol. iii. 1887-88.

otherwise be established to the age of the rock series by means of the lithological character of the specimens is thus very slight. It is probable, however, that the specimens represent series of rocks ranging in age from the Cambrian (Selkirk, Castle Mountain, and Bow River series) to the Carboniferous (Câche Creek formation), while it is not impossible that some of the less altered argillites, etc., are even referable to the Mesozoic.

The rocks which resemble most clearly those of the Cambrian of British Columbia come from the vicinity of the source of the branch of the Pelly particularly explored by Mr. Pike. No Tertiary stratified rocks or basalts such as those found in some other parts of the Yukon district occur among the specimens. The only granitic mass represented appears to be that met with in mountains on the east side of the Yus-ez-uh River, and it is notable that the granites of the Too-Tsho Range (see report already referred to) thus seem to be discontinuous to the northward.

The structure of all this northern part of the Cordilleran belt appears to be singularly irregular, and it may be a long time before it can be geologically examined in detail. The region traversed by Mr. Pike, however, evidently attaches to the northern continuation of the Selkirk, Gold, and Cariboo mountains of British Columbia rather than to the massive and comparatively unaltered limestone ranges of the Rocky Mountains proper. These, from an almost uninterrupted eastern border to the Cordillera, and in the latitudes in which Mr. Pike's exploration lay, are represented along the Mackenzie River some 150 miles to the eastward of Mr. Pike's furthest point in that direction. The intervening tract is entirely unknown both geographically and geologically.

GEORGE M. DAWSON.

II

A List of Plants collected by Mr. Warburton Pike in Alaska and the North-West Territory of Canada.

Classified by the kind assistance of Dr. Thiselton Dyer.

Anemone multifida, *DC.*
,,   ,,   ,, *var.*
,,   Richardsoni, *Hook.*
,,   parviflora, *Michx.*
Ranunculus nivalis, *L.*, *var.* Eschscholtzii.
,,   lapponicus, *L. ?*
Aquilegia brevistyla, *Hook.*
Aconitum Fischeri, *Reich.*
Papaver alpinum, *L.*
Arabis lyrata, *L. ?*
,,   retrofracta, *Graham.*
Barbarea vulgaris, *R. Br.*
Erysimum sp.
Viola palustris, *L.*
Silene acaulis, *L.*
,,   Douglasii, *Hook.*
Cerastium maximum, *L.*
,,   alpinum, *L.*
Stellaria longipes, *Goldie.*
Arenaria arctica, *Stev.*

Arenaria (merckia) physodes, *Fisch.*
Linum perenne, *L.*
Lupinus nootkatensis, *var.* borealis.
Astragalus alpinus, *L.*
    ,,   sp.
    ,,   Lambertii, *Pursh.* ?
Oxytropis splendens, *Dougl.*
    ,,   sp.
Hedysarum boreale, *Nutt.*
Dryas octopetala, *L.*
    ,,   Drummondii, *Hook.*
Rubus chamæmorus, *L.*
    ,,   arcticus, *L.*
Potentilla nivea, *L.*
    ,,   near P. Fragariastrum.
    ,,   anserina, *L.*
    ,,   fruticosa, *L.*
Rosa acicularis, *Lindl., var.*
Parnassia palustris, *L.*
Saxifraga tricuspidata, *Retz.*
Ribes hudsonianum, *Rich.*
Epilobium latifolium, *L.*
    ,,   angustifolium, *L.*
Bupleurum ranunculoides, *L.*
Cornus canadensis, *L.*
Viburnum Opulus, *L.*
Linnæa borealis, *Gron.*
Galium boreale, *L.*
Haplopappus?
Aster sibiricus, *L.*
Erigeron glaucus?
    ,,   glabellus, *Nutt., var.*
Arnica montana, *L.*
Petasites palmata, *Gray* ?

Senecio lugens, *Rich.*
Taraxacum officinalis, *Web.*, var.
Campanula sp., near C. Scheuchzeri, *Nill.*
Androsace Chamæjasme, *Host.*
Dodecatheon media, *L.*
Primula mistassinica, *Michx.*
  ,,   farinosa, *L.*
Pyrola uniflora, *L.*
  ,,   rotundifolia, *L.*
Andromeda polifolia, *L.*
Cassiope tetragona, *Don.*
Rhododendron lapponicum, *L.*
Vaccinium uliginosum, *L.*
  ,,   cæspitosum, *Michx.*
Gentiana campestris?
  ,,   prostrata, *Hænke.*
Polemonium humile, *Willd.*
Phlox subulata, *L.*
Myosotis alpestris, *Lehm.*
Mertensia sibirica, *Don.*
Pentstemon cristatus, *Nutt.*
  ,,   confertus, *Dougl.*, var. cœruleo-purpureus.
Pedicularis sudetica, *Willd.*
Utricularia intermedia, *Hayne.*
Pinguicula vulgaris, *L.*
Polygonum viviparum, *L.*
Allium Schænoprasum, *L.*
Tofieldia palustris, *Huds.*
Calla palustris, *L.*
Zygadenus glaucus, *Nutt.*
Cystopteris montana, *Bernh.*